Stonewall
Jackson

The Great Generals Series

This distinguished new series will feature the lives of eminent military leaders who changed history in the United States and abroad. Top military historians will write concise but comprehensive biographies including the personal lives, battles, strategies, and legacies of these great generals, with the aim to provide background and insight into today's armies and wars. These books will be of interest to the military history buff, and, thanks to fast-paced narratives and references to current affairs, they will be accessible to the general reader.

Patton by Alan Axelrod

Grant by John Mosier

Eisenhower by John Wukovits

LeMay by Barrett Tillman

MacArthur by Richard B. Frank

Bradley by Alan Axelrod

Andrew Jackson by Robert Remini

Stonewall Jackson

Donald A. Davis

palgrave
macmillan

First published in 2007 by
PALGRAVE MACMILLAN™
175 Fifth Avenue, New York, N.Y. 10010 and
Houndmills, Basingstoke, Hampshire, England RG21 6XS.
Companies and representatives throughout the world.

PALGRAVE MACMILLAN is the global academic imprint of the Palgrave
Macmillan division of St. Martin's Press, LLC and of Palgrave Macmillan Ltd.
Macmillan® is a registered trademark in the United States, United Kingdom
and other countries. Palgrave is a registered trademark in the European Union
and other countries.

ISBN-13: 978-1-4039-7477-8
ISBN-10: 1-4039-7477-2

Library of Congress Cataloging-in-Publication Data
Davis, Don, 1939–
    Stonewall Jackson / by Donald A. Davis.
        p.   cm. — (Great generals series)
    Includes bibliographical references and index.
    ISBN 1-4039-7477-2 (alk. paper)
    1. Jackson, Stonewall, 1824–1863.   2. Jackson, Stonewall, 1824–1863—
Military leadership   3. Generals—Confederate States of America—
Biography.   4. Confederate States of America. Army—Biography.
5. Confederate States of America. Army of Northern Virginia—Biography.
6. Mexican War, 1846–1848—Campaigns.   7. United States—History—
Civil War, 1861–1865—Campaigns.   8. Command of troops—Case studies.
9. Strategy—Case studies.   I. Title.
E467.1.J15D28   2007
973.7'3092—dc22
[B]

2007000867

Design by Letra Libre

First edition: September 2007

10   9   8   7   6   5   4   3   2   1

Printed in the United States of America.

For Karrin

Contents

Photosection appears between pages 96 and 97

Foreword

NO GENERAL EMERGED FROM THE AMERICAN CIVIL WAR WITH A more glorious reputation than Thomas "Stonewall" Jackson. His formidable skills, battlefield courage, soldierly austerity, his unforgettable nickname, his taciturn, mysterious character, and his tragic death after perhaps his greatest battle have combined to enshrine his name with the public as emblematic of that terrible conflict. But sometimes the truth is more complicated.

Donald Davis's fast-paced biography of Jackson illuminates the myths and the reality of his character and leadership, from his orphaned childhood and family relationships, through his education and early military experiences, his professorship at the Virginia Military Institute, and the full record of his Civil War leadership.

Stonewall Jackson earned his nickname for the solid performance of his brigade of troops in the First Battle of Bull Run in 1861. His Brigade didn't break under fire. And he was right there with it. But the nickname was also an appropriate tag for a man whose stubbornness and adherence to the letter of any instruction were legendary among his West Point classmates and his VMI contemporaries and cadets. Once Jackson made up his mind, there was no budging and no fudging, whether in battle or in personal relationships.

In battle he earned a worldwide reputation as the master of maneuver warfare. His 1862 campaign in the beautiful Shenandoah Valley was a masterpiece of intelligence, deception, and the just-in-time maneuver that brought success against superior forces. His 1863 flanking maneuver in the

Battle of Chancellorsville—conceived in conjunction with General Robert E. Lee—was a classic example of tactical maneuver in battle that is still studied by military students around the world.

He was also a superb trainer. He was an exacting disciplinarian, and he built strong, responsive units that were physically fit, loyal, and unquestioning in their tactical adaptability. His mastery of artillery was also a distinct plus, for he was truly a "combined-arms" trainer and commander who embedded in his units the skills and traits he had studied and observed as the most critical for success in war.

But Jackson made more than his share of mistakes, and exhibited leadership flaws that ultimately cost him his life—and perhaps the South the war. His personal recklessness was legendary. In war, commanders must take risks and be with their troops in battle, sometimes to gain intelligence, or to clinch a victory or rally their troops from defeat by their presence and personal example at decisive moments. The Civil War was the last major conflict where generals, even senior generals, were routinely forward on the battlefield. And casualties among the generals were correspondingly high. But Jackson carried risk taking to the extreme, as Davis shows, and some of it was simply unnecessary—either in his showy exhortation or his insolent over-reliance on Divine Providence. Ultimately he was killed by friendly fire when he outran his own troops in the confusion of the exploitation of his battlefield success at Chancellorsville. Lee missed him sorely, for he had no other lieutenant with his skill at seizing the initiative in battle. Had Jackson lived to command the right or left wing at Gettysburg, the Confederacy might be approaching its 150th year of independence today.

And while his penchant for extreme personal hardship—pushing himself to exhaustion, sleeping outdoors in the roughest weather, at times even refusing proper clothing and protection—set an admirable example and perhaps was the reason in part for the incredible bond he enjoyed with his troops, it also cost thousands of lives. He was simply "out" on his feet for much of the Seven Days Battle where he actually was responsible for the bulk of Lee's Army and the main effort to crush McClellan on the peninsula. Asleep, mumbling incoherently, lost, unresponsive to colleagues, his intellect and battlefield judgment failed, and the South suffered thousands of casualties while Jackson floundered. While Lee took much of the blame, and Jackson's reputation shielded him somewhat, a fresh, alert, engaged Jackson might have delivered a devastating defeat of McClellan, instead of simply pushing McClellan back toward his base.

Worse yet, it was Jackson who did this to himself, unnecessarily. Sloppy foresight and personal planning cost him several nights of essential rest. Commanders owe it to their troops to maintain their mental qualities throughout a long campaign, and must take care of themselves accordingly. It may be necessary, and even okay to push the troops so hard they're literally asleep on their feet—but for a commander to do it to himself through carelessness is just inexcusable. Today we call it "sleep discipline," and talk about it often in military training—but it is also simple common sense.

Finally, Jackson's brittle temperament—he was quick to fault others and unforgiving in response—and tendency to pick fawning friends rather than proven performers for promotion were character traits which would have been totally debilitating in higher command. Too often Lee saved him from himself.

So why read about Stonewall Jackson? To understand battle and war, to learn leadership from Jackson's successes and failures, and to ponder again the mysteries of human nature and our American heritage. For time and again we see that individual men and women do make a difference. The character, skill, competence of a single person at a crucial point can change history. Stonewall Jackson was just such a leader—and that's why you should read this book.

—*General Wesley K. Clark*

Introduction

THE DAY WAS HIS. STONEWALL JACKSON HAD SWUNG 28,000 SOL-diers out of the front line, moved them across the front of the enemy, out-flanked the Union army, and unleashed a surprise afternoon attack that utterly crushed the Federal corps on the right flank. From being static on the defensive before a superior enemy force, Jackson had seized the initiative and now held one of the most important battles of the Civil War in his hands.

As April changed to May in 1863, Union General "Fighting Joe" Hooker crossed the Rappahannock River with the Army of the Potomac, went around the Rebels entrenched at Fredericksburg, and began concen-trating the bulk of his 135,000 men near a cluster of buildings known as Chancellorsville. Robert E. Lee had about 54,000 men to stop him.

Then Hooker made the mistake of pausing in the desolate wilderness to gather his forces for the big push. This allowed time for the Confederates to catch their breath. Stonewall Jackson was sniffling from a cold when Lee joined him at a campfire in the dark hours before dawn on May 2. The South's two most aggressive leaders decided to take one of the biggest gam-bles of the war, splitting the main defensive force and letting Jackson take the rest on the dangerous sweep to find the enemy's flank.

Stonewall Jackson seldom smiled, but he had to be pleased. He was the best fighting general in the Rebel army and had spent the past two years be-deviling the Union with unorthodox tactics that led to victory after victory. A supremely modest man, the lieutenant general's name was known around the world. Federal generals always worried that he would show up where he was least expected, to do the impossible. It was his specialty, and he was about to do it again.

Shrouded in early morning mist, Jackson led his force out before dawn along a woodcutters' road not marked on any maps. Lee remained behind to keep the attention of the gathering Union forces. Incredibly, Jackson found the tip of the Union battle line totally unprepared for a fight. He calmly studied them from a hilltop as his lips moved in silent prayer and his blue eyes flashed with excitement.

At his signal, the Confederate battle lines roared down on the unsuspecting Federal encampment, bayonets gleaming in the afternoon sun and the thick woodland echoing with the Rebel yell. Wildlife fled before them, soon to be joined first by retreating pickets and skirmishers, then companies, then brigades. General Hooker did not learn of the attack until the mob of running soldiers thronged past his headquarters in panic. The entire Union XI Corps collapsed, but Stonewall Jackson kept his men moving.

He was putting into practice everything he believed as a soldier: Never let the enemy figure out what you are doing, find his weak point, strike suddenly and ruthlessly, and, once victory is procured, relentlessly pursue and crush the retreating, demoralized enemy. A major Confederate victory at Chancellorsville and the destruction of Hooker's army might change the course of the Civil War. Stonewall Jackson roamed forward with his lines, a rare look of triumph on his face.

Because of the time needed for the march, the battle did not get underway until five o'clock in the afternoon. Darkness, strong pockets of Union resistance, and confusion among Jackson's own forces on the wide, tangled battlefield eventually brought the extraordinary advance to a halt for the day.

It was a victory that would be studied for decades to come by other armies, but it was not enough for Jackson. He wanted it all. He wanted to rip Joe Hooker's Army of the Potomac to shreds, to create a victory from which the North might not be able to recover militarily, forcing it to seek a political end to the war.

To determine his next move, Jackson spurred forward on his horse Little Sorrel. With some staff members, he rode through his tired units and then beyond the forward Rebel pickets, stopping when he heard Union soldiers talking and chopping down trees. The staff members worried about the risk to their general, who was as stubborn as he was fearless, and finally coaxed him to leave the danger zone.

The group of horsemen had grown to about two dozen as they trotted back in the darkness toward safety in the Rebel lines and approached the sentries of the 18th North Carolina Regiment. The Carolina boys, who had been fighting since the start of the battle, had just tangled with a detachment of Yankee cavalry and went on alert when they heard the approaching hoof beats.

A picket opened fire at about 30 yards, and then a thick fan of musketry bloomed around the wood line and tore into Stonewall Jackson and his staff, immediately emptying many of the saddles. Jackson stayed on his horse until the shooting stopped and then was helped to the ground. He had been hit three times and lay mortally wounded. Several days later, with his left arm amputated, he died of pneumonia brought on by the wounds.

Stonewall had conquered his last battlefield, but the complexion of the war changed almost overnight. Lee would never find another commander like Jackson. Other Southern generals would finish the job at Chancellorsville and fight gallantly throughout the rest of the war, but none could match the skill and daring of that one silent, fierce, and steadfast warrior.

With Stonewall Jackson aboard Little Sorrel, the South always believed it had a chance. The same bullets that felled him pierced the heart of Dixie. Its pride shredded and its hope dimmed, the South slid into a long, dark period of battlefield losses that eventually ended in its defeat.

Jackson died for the Lost Cause of the Confederacy only to be embraced in later years as a legendary military genius and an original American hero.

CHAPTER 1

Frontier Boy

THE ATTENTION OF FOUR SMOOTH YOUNG VIRGINIA GENTLEMEN was drawn to the newcomer, who seemed remarkably out of place as he trudged to the barracks for new cadets at West Point. All four were well educated and from prosperous families, and they had the impeccable manners and polish of Old South cultured society. The new arrival was a roughhewn frontiersman awkward in his movements and wearing homespun cloth and a large slouch hat. With his big feet in old shoes, he took big strides. He had large hands calloused from hard work, and the worn saddlebags slung across his shoulder contained everything he owned.

Cadets Ambrose Powell Hill, George E. Pickett, Dabney H. Maury, and Birkett D. Fry were most taken, however, by the stern resolution in the blue eyes and stiff demeanor. A fierce determination was written on the lean face. "There was about him," Dabney Maury wrote many years later, "so sturdy an expression of purpose that I remarked, 'That fellow looks as if he had come to stay.'"[1]

All four of those cadets would become Confederate generals during the Civil War, but the peculiar young man they eyed so warily on that summer day in 1842 would outshine them all. His name was Thomas Jackson, and the world would come to know him by the nickname of "Stonewall." That first walk up from the ferry landing was an early snapshot of the kind of man and leader that Jackson would become: silent, stern, indifferent to what others thought, and caring even less about how he looked. He just moved relentlessly forward, step by step by step, until he reached his goal, be it a cadet barracks bed or a battlefield victory.

<hr />

Thomas Jackson's journey to the plains of the United States Military Academy began long before he rode the steamboat up the Hudson from New York City. His purpose there was not to become a soldier but to get the free education, lose his rough edges, and escape his heartbreaking childhood. He yearned not for military honors but for a simple life with a wife and children, professional respect, personal honor, good health, and a stable home where he could smile and laugh with close friends. The profession that would enable him to attain those things was secondary, and if soldiering had to be part of the bargain, then a soldier he would be.

His adventuresome great-grandfather, John Jackson, was born in Ireland, but of English descent, and immigrated to America in 1748 aboard a ship on which he met his future wife, Elizabeth Cummins of London. Twenty years later, they left their home in Maryland and moved the family to rural Virginia, later making the big jump across the Allegheny Mountains to the rugged wilderness that comprised the northwestern part of the state. To mark his land, John Jackson drove his tomahawk into a tree near the Buckhannon River.[2]

They had eight children. Their second boy, Edward, rose to the rank of colonel during the Revolutionary War, but his real talent was making money. He owned property by the age of 17 and eventually held thousands of acres. Successful both as a surveyor and a businessman, he established a center for his business operations and a new home, called Jackson's Mill, near Clarkston, in what is now West Virginia. Edward married twice and produced a brood of 15 children. He and his first wife, Mary Haddan, named their third child Jonathan.

Blessed with money and a worthy name, young Jonathan became a lawyer, and his family connection opened doors to success, but he did not seize those opportunities. He was a charming scoundrel who wasted his sizeable inheritance through habitual gambling and risky financial schemes, losing his land and most of his belongings except for his slaves, and one of those ran away. He did not change when he married pretty, intelligent, dark-haired Julia Neale in 1817, and before long, he was borrowing money by pledging as collateral almost everything in their three-room brick house in Clarksburg, from the butter churn to the bed. Such a casually irresponsible man would rightfully have been forgotten, but for one thing: He fathered a legend.

Julia gave birth to her first child, daughter Elizabeth, in 1819, and the first boy, Warren, came along in 1821. Details of the birth of their third child, another son, remain a mystery, which is ironic since the father was a lawyer, and the customs of the time would have dictated the recording of births and deaths in family bibles or in the courthouse right across Main Street from the family home. So, on one side or the other of midnight in the cold dark hours bridging January 20 and 21 in the year 1824, the baby boy, Thomas, was born, a blue-eyed child with fair hair. There was no middle name.

┼━━━┼

Not much is known about Stonewall Jackson's boyhood, but he learned early about the cycles of death and life. When he was only a little more than two years old, typhoid fever claimed both his six-year-old sister Elizabeth and his father. The day after her husband died, Julia Jackson gave birth to another daughter, Laura Ann.

Though Julia and her children were allowed to continue living in the house, they were almost destitute. To get by, she took in sewing and began teaching, and the family network apparently helped, as did Jonathan's fraternal brothers in the Freemasons. Then a new man swept into her life, another financially fragile Clarksburg lawyer, Blake Woodson, who had eight children of his own, although none lived with him. He and Julia married in

1830 and moved to nearby Fayette County. Soon after, she became pregnant again, and the couple made the difficult decision to send all three of Julia's children to relatives.

Warren, at age ten, was dispatched to Ohio to live with one of Julia's brothers. He became a schoolteacher and had little contact with his siblings before dying a decade later. Thomas and Laura were taken into the family at Jackson's Mill. Within just a few weeks, all three of the children were rushed back to see their mother, who was dying from complications suffered during the birth of her last child. Thomas would long remember standing beside her bed and receiving the final farewell that officially made him an orphan. It was as if his mother were abandoning him all over again.

At Jackson's Mill, in a large house beside a roaring river, Thomas and Laura found themselves in a home without want. The sawmill whined busily, chewing logs taken from the abundant Virginia forests, and the mill had spawned a number of other businesses. The matriarch was Elizabeth Brake, second wife and widow of Edward, who had found success years before after crossing the Alleghenies with his parents. A number of her unmarried children lived with her, and cousins had established homes for miles around. She owned four slaves.

The man of the house was the boisterous Cummins Jackson, a big fellow who ran the business with restless energy, brute strength, and a positive attitude. To a youth searching for a father figure, this hearty uncle seemed larger than life, and the boy admired Cummins without reservation, too young to recognize that his indulgent new hero did not belong on a pedestal. In fact, Cummins was involved in more than a few shady dealings and often demonstrated the Jackson family penchant for lawsuits. If no one else was available, the Jacksons would even sue each other. Within a few years, matriarch Elizabeth went after Cummins with a suit charging that he cheated her by trying to take over Edward's vast estate. In later years, even after he had become the famous Stonewall, Jackson never hesitated to appeal to a higher authority to get what he wanted. Even war would not change that habit.

The childhoods of Laura and Thomas continued to be shaky, for the paradise of Jackson's Mill was changing, and when deaths and marriages left little Laura as the only female in the big house, she was removed to live with an aunt in Parkersburg. An attempt was made to send ten-year-old Thomas to live with still another uncle, but the boy would have no part of that. In the past eight years, he had lost his mother, father, and a sister to death, and had watched helplessly as he was separated from his brother and now from his beloved sister Laura. He had no intention of losing Cummins, too. There might not have been the tender warmth of parental love at Jackson's Mill, but there were people there who accepted him, and that was good enough. He walked out of his foster home and returned on foot to the mill, demonstrating the stubbornness and determination that would mark his entire life.

Thomas flourished under the steady hard regimen of physical work, with plenty of friends and neighbors and the daily frontier routine. He worked the at the mill, cut wood, did chores, labored in the fields, worked with the slaves, and rode as a jockey for Cummins at the races on his uncle's own four-mile track. A tendency toward illness was countered by the outdoor exercise.

At West Point, the homesick cadet wrote longingly to Laura that he was enjoying himself, but felt "deprived of the blessings of a home, the society of the friends of my child-hood, the cordial welcome of relatives and above all the presence of an only sister. Times are now far different from what they once were. Once I was in my native state at my adopted home none to give there mandates none for me to obey but as I chose surrounded by my playmates and natives all apparently eager to promote my happiness."[3]

⊹⊱━⊰⊹

Strangely, the two things that Jackson would prize above almost all else as an adult, education and religion, were missing in those early days. Education was the key to bettering himself, and once he began to learn, he never stopped. And the adult Jackson would proudly practice his stern religious views no matter where he was. But in childhood, both were almost absent as formative influences.

His mother was a devout Christian, and any child raised where he was would have done what all of his friends did, what everyone he knew did: go to church on the Sabbath. It was part of life, just like harvesting crops, tending the animals, and sawing logs.

Education had to compete with field work. Teachers in small communities did what they could with a limited number of available days, but imparted little more than the basics of reading and writing. Thomas was good at sports, and popular with his mates, but he received, at best, an unremarkable education. Nevertheless, outside of the classroom, he was learning the hard lessons of life and developing an extremely solid character. Unlike his father, this was a lad who meant what he said, could be trusted on a handshake deal, was generous and protective, and could be depended upon to get a tough job done.

When he was 17, those characteristics and family connections helped him get a job as a Lewis County constable, carrying out duties appropriate for a deputy sheriff. The habit of being precise and exact when collecting outstanding debts and serving warrants taught him the value of paying close attention to detail and numbers.

Deep down, Thomas Jackson wanted more out of life, although he did not know exactly what. He knew only the towns of his small part of Virginia, but his explorations showed him there was a big world out there, and his extended family taught him that self-reliance could take a young man far. But where? And how?

His father and stepfather had both been lawyers, and he had come in contact with many successful men who had the advantage of an education beyond that of a rustic schoolroom. If he did not want to be tied to the mill, farm, and plow, Thomas had to expand his limited universe of knowledge. One day in early 1842, when he was 19, he learned that his district's congressman, Representative Samuel Lewis Hays, had to fill an opening at the United States Military Academy. The position offered a free university education, and Thomas decided to go after it.

He knew he did not have the formal schooling expected of someone seeking entry to a major university that stressed mathematics and engineering. Obstacles never deterred Jackson. He believed in himself, but with a realistic self-examination of his ability. "I am very ignorant," he admitted in one discussion. "But I know I have the energy and I think I have the intellect."[4]

Jackson was among four applicants in the district, but one dropped out because he was below the minimum age, leaving three. Two of Thomas's friends were also applying, one of them a young man who worked as a clerk for the county. The competitive examination would be overseen by Captain

George Washington Jackson, a member of the widespread family. The captain remained neutral, and Gibson Butcher, the courthouse clerk, was appointed on April 19, 1842. Butcher, who was nimble with numbers, took top score, only to be absolutely startled by what he found upon arriving at West Point: rigorous discipline, harsh treatment, and onerous duties among strangers, far from Virginia. Only a day after arriving at West Point on June 4, he left the military academy without even informing Congressman Hays.

Making his way home, Butcher stopped at Jackson's Mill and told Thomas of his decision. The original field of four applicants was now down to two, Thomas and his friend Joe Lightburn, but because of the stakes, friendship could stand in the way. This time the family decided to go into action, and Cummins, the other uncles, family friends, and Captain Jackson, who no longer had to stay neutral, launched a campaign to get Thomas into the open slot. Letters of recommendation were drafted, and numerous signatures were gathered from people who knew the congressman, including Hays's own son, Peregrine Hays, another of Thomas's good friends.

Jackson dashed to Washington by horseback, stagecoach, and train and showed up at the congressman's office, where he handed Hays Gibson Butcher's resignation letter along with a thick bundle of documents recommending him to Hays. The question of his lack of formal schooling was balanced by the boy's steely determination. The next day, June 17, Thomas J. Jackson was appointed to be a cadet at the United States Military Academy. [5]

It was the first time that the initial "J" showed up in correspondence, and Jackson never said what it stood for or used a full middle name. Over time, the assumption became that it stood for the name of his father, Jonathan. No one knows.

He did not have to be at the academy for several more weeks, so Hays invited him to spend a few days in Washington. Thomas declined. The congressman introduced him to the secretary of war, who approved the appointment, but gave Thomas an inkling of how the frontier boy might be received by others at the spit-and-polish military school, offering this bit of advice: "Sir, you have a good name. Go to West Point, and the first man who insults you, knock him down, and have it charged to my account!"[6]

CHAPTER 2

West Point

THE WEST POINT CLASS OF 1846 BEGAN WITH 123 ARRIVALS AS first-year cadets. This number dwindled with the academic and physical tests that preceded formal induction. Thomas Jackson was among the 93 survivors.

Then came summer camp, a mind-numbing experience that immersed the raw cadets in the military lifestyle. Still in civilian clothes, they learned to march, to stay in step and keep a rank dressed, to stand at attention, and to salute. Orders were to be obeyed instantly, and they sweated through exercise and menial chores designed to fatigue and anger them and to teach them discipline. Jackson would always remember his own days as a green beginner and emphasize that his soldiers had to be trained hard before they could be expected to fight.

During those hot summer months, there was little the cadets could do correctly in the eyes of their upperclassmen tormentors, who mocked Jackson as "the General" for having the same last name as the former President Andrew Jackson, the hero of the War of 1812. [1] He would not have been bothered by someone yelling in his face, for he had grown up surrounded by energetic, rowdy men, and was often pushed to his physical limits. He was shy and quiet, a bit older than the average plebe and so obviously capable of standing up for himself that he apparently was not bothered as much as some of his weaker classmates. His troubled childhood had instilled a solid confidence in his self-worth. Jackson had survived things a lot worse than summer camp. Try as they might, the camp leaders could not rattle the dour Virginian. Dabney Maury tried to play a joke. Jackson was on an evening detail picking up trash when Maury, also a plebe, raised his tent flap and barked at him to work harder. Jackson stared back silently with his penetrating blue eyes, and Maury later attempted to "humble" himself and apologize. He said, "Mr. Jackson, I find that I made a mistake just now in speaking to you in a playful manner not justified by our slight acquaintance. I regret that I did so."

Jackson stiffly replied, "That is perfectly satisfactory, sir." He made no further overture. Maury had been rebuffed in an earlier attempt to befriend Jackson, and was at his wit's end with the man. "Cadet Jackson of Virginia is a jackass," he declared to his tent mates. [2]

⊹══⊨══⊹

Fall came, as did the uniforms, and Jackson turned into a soldier. His posture had already improved by the time he proudly took his place among the corps of cadets. Harsh hazing, physical demands, and the rough life of summer camp had been endured and overcome, but he now had to face his hardest challenge—the classroom.

Congress had established the United States Military Academy in 1802 on the high west bank of the Hudson River, fifty miles north of New York City, in order to create a professional army for the changing young nation. By the time Thomas Jackson entered West Point, tribes of Native Americans were being resettled into the sparse territories out west, and an intrepid young explorer named John Charles Frémont, a West Pointer, was about to blaze a trail beyond the Mississippi into the promise of the distant Oregon territories. Relations were very strained between the United States and Mexico over the future of Texas. Trouble, in some form, would certainly come in the future, and there would be a need for trained officers.

Jackson was one of many beneficiaries of the radical decision by Congress to trade a free college education in exchange for a term of active army service. It was a godsend for many talented but poor young men, who were blended with the sons of landed gentry to create a talent pool which grew larger each year. Even if they drifted back into civilian life, a West Point graduate skilled in military basics would be able to step into a position of leadership if called back to duty.

When the Civil War erupted almost two decades after the Class of 1846 began its academic journey, West Pointers became a treasured commodity and reached senior positions on both sides; many would wear generals' stars before that war was done. Of the 60 battles fought during the conflict, graduates of the United States Military Academy were on both sides of 55 of them, and a West Point graduate commanded one of the opposing sides in the remaining five.[3] At Appomattox, Robert E. Lee, Class of '29, surrendered to Ulysses S. Grant, Class of '43.

West Point emphasized mathematics, and the highest honor awarded at graduation was a commission in the Army Corps of Engineers. Jackson's brilliant classmate George McClellan, who was only 15 years old when he entered West Point with two years of college already behind him, admitted that the academy did not require him to study much. Jackson was at the other end of that line, for his backwoods schoolwork had not adequately prepared him for the challenge of university-level math. Even things as simple as fractions gave him trouble. Working on a problem at a blackboard, he would sweat profusely as chalk dust flew about, but no matter how hard he tried, the answers eluded him, his grades sank, and the rankings were merciless. He only squeaked by in the daily exams, trudging in slow cadence with other "Immortals," cadets of such low academic standing that their futures were in jeopardy.

Cadet Jackson simply would not surrender. His sole resource was to work even harder, and he attacked his books with the same inflexible determination that would mark his entire military career. He could overcome any challenge, if he just worked hard enough! While others slept, Jackson stacked coal in the tiny grate that warmed his small room and lay before the unsteady glare for hours, studying.

He eventually came upon an unusual system that worked for him: refusing to move at the pace of everyone else. Jackson would not take on a new problem until he had completely conquered the previous one and had imprinted the solution on his brain. He did not worry about being marked down in class the next day for being unprepared for the newest equations, and he slowly built the wall of numbers, brick by brick, and mastered every one. It kept him afloat until other cadets began to help, the grades improved, and he moved out of the dubious company of the Immortals. By the end of his first year, although not academically distinguished, neither was he disgraced. Once again, Jackson survived.

"You can be whatever you resolve to be," Jackson wrote in a private notebook. Looking back on it more than a century later, it was a picture of the inner man. These rules of life, his "maxims," rolled off his pen in perfect tune with his growing confidence, as he instructed himself to be frugal, industrious, and quiet, to accept few close friends and not to worry about "trifles" and accidents. Above all, do what you say you are going to do, and "sacrifice your life rather than your word."

The biblical Ten Commandments were not among his maxims, indicating that the fervid Christianity that eventually would guide him had not yet taken root during his time at West Point.

Other cadets watched in wonder when they saw him at study, for he sat stiffly erect before the book and papers on his table, hardly aware of anything other than the lesson, lost in intense focus. His eyes would lock onto a spot on the ceiling or the wall, and he would remain almost hypnotically motionless while his busy brain unlocked some problem. "No one I have ever known could so perfectly withdraw his mind from surrounding objects or influences, and so thoroughly involve his whole being in the subject under consideration," said one former roommate. "To make the author's knowledge his own was ever the point at which he aimed." [4]

In future years, the habit disconcerted people who mistook the silence and standoffish behavior as indications that Jackson was unaware of what was happening around him. During the First Battle of Bull Run, an artillery officer arrived on the active battlefield and found Jackson sitting against a tree with his cap pulled low on his brow, seemingly immobile. He asked the general where to place his unit, and barely moving his lips, Jackson plugged the new troops into exactly the correct position on the line. The general's body might catch a brief rest, but not his mind.

Jackson's improvement at West Point was steady, and his academic standing rose. Although he tamed his classroom demons in math, other parts of the curriculum still posed challenges. He did not possess the correct "seat" on a horse expected of a true cavalryman, for he had grown up around work animals, not thoroughbreds. Fencing, a useless course in the age of guns, would have been a struggle for such an ungainly person. Jackson also had difficulty with the drawing classes, which were required because an engineer had to turn observations into maps and plans. Although he never acquired great skills in drawing, he absorbed the importance of the lesson the classes were meant to teach and had a personal mapmaker during the war.

His most pleasant surprise was the discovery of a course in which he could excel and not merely survive. Everything Thomas Jackson had—the meticulously logical mind, the personal demand for perfection—came into play the day he walked into a class called "natural and experimental philosophy." Here, the other cadets had trouble, but not Jackson. It was the realm of science where reason ruled, and he devoured lessons on everything from physics to astronomy.

The conduct of war, famous battles, tactics, and strategy were not emphasized at West Point during that era, and it was not until his senior year that Jackson was finally exposed to classes on the military arts and sciences, such as fortifications and artillery and infantry tactics. The courses were not deep, and none of his instructors detected that the dogged, studious Jackson might have any special aptitude in the subjects.

In addition to sharpening his mind and honing his body into an impressive military presence, Jackson approached the end of his four years at West Point having learned something else of immense value. A true officer was expected to be able to handle a dinner engagement, to dance and carry on polite conversation at social gatherings. Jackson, the rustic, had to learn most of those graces from scratch, but he mastered these lessons, too, and became comfortable in a new skin of quiet, disciplined civility. He had spent four years in New York learning to become a Southern gentleman.

That did not mean the rough frontiersman had become a pushover. Once, another cadet stole Jackson's musket and replaced it with a dirty one. Young Jackson erupted in a firestorm when he discovered his clean firearm had vanished. He was beyond anger, for the theft was a betrayal of the high degree of trust cadets had been taught. Also, it was *his* musket, which made it a personal matter.

The muskets carried no serial numbers, but Jackson could identify his weapon by a unique marking, and at a special inspection, it was found in the possession of an unruly cadet from Missouri. The mystery was solved, but Jackson fell back upon the stormy habits of his litigious family and demanded that the thief be court-martialed and thrown out of the academy. Eventually, he was persuaded to let the matter go, but it was an example of how this man, logical and even-tempered to the extreme, could still detonate into unreasoning rage over what he perceived as a personal affront.

+≻═≺+

Thomas J. Jackson graduated in 1846, ranked in the upper third of his class of 59 cadets. Because of his steady progress upward, some believed if the course had lasted a few years longer, he would have risen to the top. Many of the graduates of that year would become generals in the Civil War and fight against classmates and old friends.

As was customary, Jackson received the rank of brevet second lieutenant and was assigned to the artillery. He would have to wait for an opening in the active duty ranks to officially become a second lieutenant.

Against incredible odds, the boy from the backwoods of Virginia had become an officer and a gentleman of the U.S. Army.

CHAPTER 3

Artilleryman

SIMMERING TENSION BETWEEN MEXICO AND THE UNITED STATES boiled over when the Republic of Texas, independent for almost ten years, was admitted to the Union as the twenty-eighth state at the end of 1845. Mexico still claimed the rich territory, and when diplomacy failed to resolve the problem, General Zachary Taylor occupied Point Isabel, and Mexican troops ambushed a detachment of American dragoons. In May 1846, a month after Brevet Second Lieutenant Thomas Jackson left West Point, the United States declared war.

It would prove to be much more than a war for Jackson, for it was in Mexico that he discovered what a fighting army was all about. It was the best classroom in the world. He would receive a fighting man's dirt-level view of many of the kind of tactics, decisions, and maneuvers that would make him famous during the Civil War, and it was there that he first became a hero.

Mexico thought it could win the war with its large army, but the Americans were superior from the start. The United States moved a large force into the far west against the Mexican troops in California and New Mexico, and a second force, under Zachary Taylor, pushed into Mexico itself.

That plunge across the border was successful, but it left the Americans still more than 600 miles from the ultimate prize of Mexico City, capital of the Republic, which was located in the middle of the country. Obstacles of all sorts, from mountains to deserts, blocked easy movement, and a multitude of fortified towns and cities promised bloody fighting for any advance. It would be almost impossible to maintain a decent supply tail all the way back to the United States. The decision was made to leave Taylor campaigning through northern Mexico and create still a third force under the command of General Winfield Scott, one of the most experienced officers in the army, to stage an amphibious assault on the coastal city of Vera Cruz, about 250 miles east of Mexico City. Jackson would be part of that push.

╪══•══╪

He had reported for duty with Company K, 1st Artillery, at Fort Hamilton, New York, a unit already under assignment to move to Mexico. Thirty-six days after leaving New York and undertaking an arduous trip by foot, riverboat, and ship, they arrived off Point Isabel, their ships pitching in a September storm. But the target of Monterrey had already fallen, so after several weeks Company K went aboard the boats again, heading up the Rio Grande to join the assault on Saltillo, capital of the border state of Coahuila. Saltillo gave up without a fight. Moving men, guns, horses, wagons and supplies over great distances was a challenging and dirty business, and Jackson, as acting quartermaster, performed his duties well, but he did not catch up with the early fighting. "How I should like to be in *one* battle!" he would grump to a friend, revealing the anxiety of an untested young officer. [1]

In March, new orders put Jackson's company aboard a sailing ship as part of the 13,000-man force that General Scott took on a gigantic flanking movement, a 160-mile sweep down the eastern coast of Mexico. More than 200 ships stayed out of sight of land as they sailed across the Tropic of Cancer and deep into the Gulf of Campeche before swinging in and dropping anchor near Vera Cruz. Bands played loudly from the decks of the big ships as the attack detachments loaded into longboats, and sailors pulled their oars. Knots of curious civilians in small boats paddled among them.

A mirror-smooth sea and a gentle southeast breeze aided the landing, and with no opposition, the U.S. soldiers came ashore safely. Within six hours, they had set up defensive positions along the beach, with the white walls of Vera Cruz visible only a few miles away. Scott laid a tight siege to isolate the city, which could no longer be reinforced and had enough supplies for only a few weeks. [2]

+≈═≈+

The general decided to use the most economical way of taking the city, simply pounding it into submission. American artillery pieces, including some huge naval guns that had been brought ashore, were emplaced in positions selected by Captain Robert E. Lee, who would distinguish himself throughout the campaign.

For three days, the cannons thundered through gaps in walls of sandbags stacked taller than a man's head along the beach dunes, drilling shots that arced over palm trees and scrub brush to explode in the gleaming white city. Shock waves battered the men firing the huge guns, and they choked in drifting, ground-clinging clouds of acrid smoke and dust as they constantly reloaded, aimed, and fired. Balloons of smoke and flashes of fire blossomed in the distance as the Mexican artillery answered, and cannon balls flew past the men and Jackson, one coming within five feet of him.

His thirst for a fight was slaked and a dormant genius was awakened, for he found that he was comfortable in battle, calm and able to move purposefully among the guns, working in tune to the hammering metronome of artillery fire. He was not afraid.

The Mexican government was in shambles, and the one-legged war hero General Antonio López de Santa Anna, conqueror of the Alamo, was brought back from exile to assume the presidency. He moved strongly against Zachary Taylor in northern Mexico at Buena Vista, but lost that battle despite outnumbering the Americans almost three-to-one. That left him not only defeated at Buena Vista, but totally out of position to help Vera Cruz hundreds of miles away. With no relief possible and under steady bombardment, the Vera Cruz garrison surrendered. American flags were hoisted over both the city and the huge harbor castle fortress of San Juan d'Ulloa.

Jackson had tasted battle, distinguishing himself and banishing forever any concern that he might not be up to the task. He would never worry about getting shot.

+≡≡≡+

Several weeks passed as Scott organized the overland lunge for Mexico City. On April 8, the first American columns pushed out of Vera Cruz and into the foothills of the treacherous Sierra Madre Oriental mountains, taking the same steep road believed to have once been used by the soldiers of Hernando Cortez. To reach Jalapa some 65 miles away, the Americans had to traverse a 10,000-foot-high pass at Cerro Gordo, which Santa Anna had turned it into a mountain fortress. A deep chasm with rugged cliffs secured the right flank, and thousands of troops defended the craggy crest on the left. Artillery covered the climbing, winding road of sharp turns and switchbacks, making a frontal assault impossible.

Although not working together, both Robert E. Lee and Jackson were soaking up tactical lessons they would use together to great effect in their future battlefield partnership. An important one was: Avoid the enemy's strength and spring an attack on his weakest point. Engineers led by Captain Lee found an approach among the cliffs and crags that Santa Anna believed impregnable, and within three days, a rough road was built without the Mexican sentries catching a glimpse of what was happening. The Americans came up, moving hand over hand up cliffs so sheer that the animals could not make it and had to be left behind. Dismantled artillery pieces were hoisted on ropes by muscle power.

They attacked the Mexican flank at dawn on April 18, catching the defenders by surprise. Artillerymen joined the infantry charges, and the unexpected attack on the right flank broke the Mexican defense and sent those troops reeling in confusion, pushing chaos onto the other defenders until the whole Cerro Gordo position collapsed. The Americans pursued the retreating Mexicans back so fast that Santa Anna himself barely escaped in time, taking off on a mule in such a hurry that he had to abandon his wooden leg.

One Mexican general was killed and five more were captured, about 1,200 Mexican troops were slain or wounded, and another 3,000 taken prisoner. Forty-three bronze artillery pieces that had been cast in Spain were captured. The Americans lost 431 men killed and wounded, including two generals.

Jackson was promoted to the full rank of second lieutenant and cited for gallant and meritorious service. The promotion came with a new assignment to a company manning heavier guns, but now that Jackson had a taste for combat, he did not want to be left out. Deliverance came when he heard that Captain John Magruder had been given command of a full four-gun Mexican artillery field battery that he had captured. Jackson pounced on the opportunity. "I bent all my energies to be with him, for I knew if any fighting was to be done, Magruder would be on hand," he would observe later. [3] He became part of Magruder's highly maneuverable team, Company I of the 1st Artillery, which was expressly designed to get some guns into a fight in a hurry.

Following the clearing of Cerro Gordo, the advance moved inland as one Mexican position after another gave up without a fight. After Jalapa, the castle of Perote surrendered, then the large city of Puebla, offering no resistance. Once in Puebla, Scott stopped for a month to reorganize, only 80 miles from Mexico City.

The string of victories carried the seed of a potential disaster, however, for the general found himself in the middle of Mexico with a vulnerable supply road extending back through the mountains to the ships at Vera Cruz. His daring answer was to sever those connections entirely, leave the sick and wounded in Puebla, and push his main force of around 10,000 men as fast as possible through the remaining range of mountains.

Santa Anna was waiting in Mexico City with 30,000 defenders and artillery pieces covering every approach. Scott's soldiers climbed the last high mountain ridges and finally saw the metropolis glittering below. It was a tactical nightmare. The roads bristled with enemy fortifications, lakes and marshes limited movement, and a forbidding plain of sharp volcanic rock and huge boulders, called the Pedregal, loomed as a natural trap.

Once again, Captain Lee's engineers found some rude paths that could be made just usable enough to pass men and guns across in order to reach a better road extending behind the fortified village of Contreras. That gave General Scott two possible approaches, about seven miles apart, and although mutual support was impossible, he chose to move on both.

Among those crossing the desolate Pedregal was the four-gun artillery battery of Captain Magruder, including Lieutenant Jackson, and a supporting battery of howitzers. The guns had to be wrestled through the rocks, and Mexican heavy artillery commanded the area. A number of horses and men of the battery, including its senior lieutenant, were killed. Magruder appointed Jackson to take over the position, and although he could not actually see Jackson because of a storm and the bad terrain, he could hear Jackson's guns barking steadily, moving forward when Magruder did. Magruder would mention him favorably in his official report. After hours of battle, during which Mexican infantrymen and cavalry charges tried to storm the brittle American positions, enough reinforcements arrived to steady the line and allow the battered artillerymen to fall back.

Santa Anna moved 12,000 men forward to crush the Americans, but the U.S. commanders were not about to allow him to dictate the battlefield, another important lesson in Jackson's life. Leaving a few regiments in a blocking position, they swung out on another flanking movement, as Captain Lee again picked a path through the volcanic debris. At daybreak, they smashed through the astonished defenders of the Contreras line, and once again the Mexicans dissolved and fell back in demoralized chaos as the Americans charged forward after them. In a simultaneous major battle, the other American force stormed into the fortifications of Churubusco. The battles cost Santa Anna almost 4,300 dead and wounded, and another few thousand were taken prisoner. General Scott lost 137 American dead and 877 wounded, along with 38 men missing. Cut off from resupply, those were casualties that Scott could not replace.

Scott offered a truce, and Santa Anna treacherously used time he had been given to consider the offer to reassemble his army once again, establish more positions, and then reject the armistice.

One cannot assume that Jackson was taking notes on tactics, but he was obviously soaking up important military lessons from a front-line perspective in the dirt. Many future Civil War generals were getting hands-on demonstrations on such things as rapid flanking movements, the way to block superior forces with shrewd defense, the value of well-placed artillery, the need for bold offensive action and unexpected attacks, the contagious bravery that comes from soldiers fighting in desperate circumstances, and the importance of never giving the enemy a chance to recover. The bold application of those lessons would become Stonewall Jackson's trademark in a future war.

General Scott resumed his offensive on September 8 at the town of Molino del Rey, but the attacking American force of only 500 men was turned back with heavy casualties, and Mexican troops speared the wounded. A cavalry attack threatened to flank the survivors, until the guns of Magruder and Jackson rumbled to the scene and blew apart their charge. The Americans took the town, but the battle shrank Scott's force down to only 7,500 effective men, with the strongpoint of Chapultapec, a fortified castle, looming above them and Mexico City still to be captured.

Jackson's artillery section was attached, under his independent command, to a pair of infantry regiments that set off on a route around the northern side of the big castle on September 13. Jackson pushed his men and horses so hard that it was too late by the time he realized that they had outpaced their infantry support, and Mexican guns opened up on them. When progress was hampered by a ditch, his troops were caught in a hail of cannon and infantry fire as they manhandled one gun across and got it firing. The soldiers dove for cover, but Jackson needed them to get up and fight. He would later write that, although he believed thousands of muskets were shooting at him, he walked around in the open, saying to his hiding men, "See, there is no danger. I am not hit." [4]

A sergeant responded to help fight the single gun, then Magruder arrived, a second gun was put into action, and they knocked out the Mexican battery in a close-range duel. The American infantry scaled the walls and captured the castle, taking bloody revenge for the Americans who had been bayoneted on the ground at Molino del Ray.

Jackson and other American gunners suddenly had a shooting gallery open before them, and they hurled a continual barrage into the throngs of Mexican troops retreating toward Mexico City with the U.S. infantry close behind. All of the close work among the loud cannons during the war permanently damaged his hearing.

Jackson had again proved that he possessed a soldier's courage, and his name showed up in glowing reports from several senior commanders. He was promoted to a regular first lieutenant and given the brevet rank of captain for his fighting at Contreras. The bravery and success at Chapultepec won him another promotion to brevet major.

The true assessment of his work, however, came when General Scott threw a party in the National Palace in Mexico City to celebrate the final victory. One by one, officers passed politely before the general, who genially shook their hands. The line came to a halt when Thomas Jackson stepped before him.

"I don't know that I shall shake hands with Mr. Jackson," declared the general, in solemn tones. He had drawn himself stiff, a most imposing figure at six feet five inches tall, put his hands behind his back and, stared at the Virginian as the hall fell silent.

Jackson was thunderstruck, having no idea how he had offended the commanding general.

Scott spoke loudly: "If you can forgive yourself for the way you slaughtered all those Mexicans, I'm not sure I can!" Then he broke into a big smile and grabbed the hand of the shaken young artilleryman.

CHAPTER 4

Quitting the Army

THE PARTY AT THE NATIONAL PALACE WAS BUT A TASTE OF THE good life available to the conquering army's troops in Mexico. While the guns cooled and diplomats haggled in lengthy peace negotiations, the Mexicans, weary of war and revolution, proved to be gracious hosts.

Until then, Jackson's life had been one of demanding self-sacrifice and hard work, with little time for anything other than the task before him. The bleak childhood in an extreme rural environment was followed by years of arduous study at West Point, and then he was plunged straight into a war. In Mexico, at peace, Jackson was forced by circumstance to discover that life could also be pleasant.

At twenty-three years old, he was an honored officer and a carefully trained gentleman. He stood about five feet ten, with dark brown hair and a new beard on his handsome, hawk-like face. The slender frame was sculpted by hard work and a careful diet.

Jackson was welcome at frequent social functions. He paid $180 for a splendid horse, took care to dress properly in his blue uniform, studied Spanish, and sought lessons on how to polish his manners—which he called "graces"—even more. When a day of duty was done, Jackson fell easily into the Mexican custom of strolling the beautiful Paseo after dinner, watching the attractive women and the carriages of the elite go by. His letters hinted at exotic romance. "I think I shall probably spend many years here and (though I have not done so yet) to make my life more natural by sharing it with some amiable Señorita," he wrote to his sister. [1] The young officer from backwoods Virginia was totally smitten by the country he had helped defeat. Until the end of his days, Jackson's favorite term of endearment for his wife would be the Spanish term *esposa*.

━━━━━━

With its fertile ground and temperate weather, Mexico teemed with tropical plants and bushes and vibrant flowers. Fountains spouted clear water in cosmopolitan city squares. Jackson frequently dined on fruit picked fresh from the trees and vegetables carted into the city from the rich farmlands. He found it all very agreeable to his health.

Jackson had strange and strong habits and convictions about his medical condition. At West Point, he would sit rigidly erect in his chair to study because he believed such a posture would keep his internal organs safely aligned, rather than have them pressing against each other as when the body was bent. He would sometimes hold his left arm straight up for long periods to keep blood from rushing uselessly from his heart to an extremity that was not in use. One side of his body might feel heavier than the other. Horseback riding aided the digestion. He would not smoke or drink spirits. Headaches, colds, aches, and pains assumed greater importance to him, as did perceived cures, and within a few years, Dabney Maury would observe that Jackson "had become hypochondratical [*sic*] . . . [with] queer ideas about his health." [2] Some of his ailments, such as dyspepsia, eye strain, and hearing loss were both real and troublesome.

Oddly, the Mexican War actually seemed to improve Jackson's health, possibly because he ate better and exercised more, but also because he did not have as much time during combat to worry about little things that might, or might not, be going on inside his body. In his letters from both Vera Cruz and Jalapa to his sister Laura, he confirmed that he was feeling very well.

For a man who worried so much about being frail, it is odd that Jackson survived Mexico at all. In the tropical zone during an era of primitive medical care, the unsanitary conditions, bad water, bad hygiene, and poor rations left sick men crowded together in encampments where illness spread at alarming rates. About 2,000 U.S. servicemen died during the Mexican War from combat wounds, while more than 11,500 died from diseases that included virulent yellow fever, malaria, measles, and dysentery. Another 10,000 received disability discharges, and many of these died before they got back home. More would pass away at an early age. Disease slaughtered many more Americans than did the Mexican army. [3]

Yet amid some of the most deadly diseases known to man, Jackson was not one of the thousands who ended up wrapped in a blanket and buried in a shallow grave in a foreign land. Not only did he survive, he thrived!

Jackson considered himself a Christian, but he had not gone regularly to church until West Point, where he and other cadets attended chapel. In Mexico, he began to seriously consider allowing religion into his life.

Colonel Francis Taylor, the commander of the 1st Artillery, was a devout Episcopalian who took time to instruct his young officers about religion and to pray with them. Lieutenant Jackson of Company K was more than interested in what Taylor had to say in those sessions, which took place during the long hours of inactivity that precede and follow any battle. Jackson took to heart Taylor's suggestion to study the Bible, but did so absent the emotion of religious conversion. He attacked the Scripture as if memorizing math tables.

He wanted to learn more before choosing any faith and was fascinated by the imprint of the Catholic Church in Mexico. There was a church in almost every village, and worshippers removed their hats in respect even when just passing by. But he was puzzled by such things as the gilded interior of a cathedral in Jalapa and the elaborate robes of priests when so many of their followers were poor.

Jackson threw himself into investigating the possibilities of the Roman Catholic faith with the same diligence he applied in studying everything else. He even lived for a period with a group of priests, who helped him obtain an interview with the archbishop of Mexico City. He was intensely curious and serious, but he did not convert. Jackson would leave Mexico still unbaptized, still uncommitted, still searching for a religious home.

+===+

Mexico had been rewarding for Jackson's professional career and private life, but the period began to close when the peace treaty was signed on February 2, 1848. A firm border was established, but the true prize was the land ceded to the United States, some 525,000 square miles that stretched all the way to the Pacific Ocean. The territory, which encompasses present-day California, Arizona, New Mexico, Utah, and western Colorado, was wrapped into the agreement, and Texas was secure. The path to America's westward expansion was clear. The United States paid $15 million and excused Mexico from about $3 million in claims from U.S. citizens.

It was time for Brevet Major First Lieutenant Thomas Jackson and his fellow soldiers to go home, and within eight months, he was back in New York, reporting at Fort Columbus, a red brick citadel shaped like a star that dominated the northern end of Governors Island, only some 500 yards from the southern end of Manhattan. He took a leave during the autumn to visit his family in Virginia, where he spent time with Laura and discovered that California gold fever had gripped the rambunctious clan in Jackson's Mill. Uncle Cummins was heading out to dig his fortune; in little more than a year, he would perish in pursuit of that dream.

On his return to New York, Jackson was assigned to Fort Hamilton, a top posting for an artilleryman, for it bristled with thirty 32-pounder cannons and 14 other big guns and was part of the city's harbor defense cordon. It occupied a section of what is now the southwestern corner of Brooklyn and eventually became one of the anchor sites of the Verrazano-Narrows Bridge. There, he settled into the monotonous routines of a peacetime officer, including making trips to other installations as a member of courts martial panels, a task he undertook with the utmost seriousness. He still attended parties, enjoyed the company of attractive women, and walked the wide streets of New York City, where, he said, a person could find everything but peace and quiet.

Then he found religion. Still under the influence of his fatherly commanding officer, Francis Taylor, Jackson attended church every Sunday and prayed by himself every day. Six months after arriving at Fort Hamilton, he was baptized in St. John's Episcopal Church on an April Sunday in 1849.

His restless soul may have been placated, but things were not otherwise well with Jackson. In constant financial trouble, at one point he was down to having only ten dollars to his name. Cold and wet weather had settled over Virginia during his return from leave, and New York was moving into a frigid winter. His illnesses were now very real: the aches of rheumatism, aching feet sensitive to the cold, and eye problems plagued. He fought back with visits to doctors, did up to three hours a day of hard exercise, such as chopping wood, and ate a meager diet so strict that he would carry his own food, such as pieces of stale bread, to fancy soirees, disdaining the host's wine in order to drink plain water. Tea, broiled meat, egg yolks, and some but not all vegetables were on his food list. As with everything, once Jackson set himself a particular course, he went all the way.

He adopted "water cures" to ease his ailments. These included both soaking in hot pools and drinking great quantities of water, particularly if it contained minerals he thought were healthful. And just as he had managed to avoid serious disease in Mexico, Jackson was untouched when a cholera epidemic swept New York, killing 4,000 people.

<hr />

After two years at Fort Hamilton, Jackson was transferred into a new company that was sent just before Christmas in 1850 to the dank wilderness of Fort Meade, a sandy, scrubby outpost in the middle of central Florida, not far above the Everglades.

Out on the wooded trails, leading scouting parties, Jackson was fine. It was a joy to be doing something useful, marching his troops hard for 30 miles or more, inculcating in them the same habit of traveling fast that would distinguish his Civil War soldiers. The Indian Wars were over, so while there was little danger, there was trouble in another form.

Jackson, a first lieutenant, and his commanding officer, William Henry French, a captain, fell to arguing about who was in charge of construction at the fort. Typically, Jackson jumped into the situation with both boots and made matters immeasurably worse. What happened next makes sense only if viewed through the prism of his family's penchant for lawsuits and his own earlier reaction during the West Point dirty musket incident.

Nothing would appease the brooding Jackson, who refused to speak to the captain unless it was militarily necessary. It seemed that the good of the service was secondary, as everything he had learned on the battlefields of Mexico faded in importance during a personal tiff with another officer who proved just as stubborn and picky as he.

When Jackson appealed to a general, he was rejected out of hand. This caused him to lapse into a morose anger and begin a private investigation to prove Captain French was having an extramarital affair with a servant girl. He charged French with conduct unbecoming an officer, and French responded by having Jackson arrested on similar charges. The little world of Fort Meade started to come apart at the seams as French and Jackson, both brevet majors, flailed at each other. The appeal process released Jackson from arrest, and both officers were told to stop squabbling. French filed still another appeal to get Jackson tried, but Jackson went on an extended leave while the paperwork was sent to Washington. The affair soared all the way up to Winfield Scott, who had become the top general in the army and was not amused by the behavior of two heroes from the Mexican campaign. Jackson received a stern reprimand.

It was a wicked course that Thomas Jackson had pursued, and it would not be the last of his reckless attacks. During the Civil War, he would place some competent generals under arrest and force others out of the army.

By the time General Scott returned his decision, Thomas Jackson had already made up his own mind to leave. Back on February 25, 1851, he had accepted an offer to be considered for a teaching position at the Virginia Military Institute in Lexington, Virginia. The next month, was accepted by the VMI Board of Visitors to become professor of natural and experimental philosophy and professor of artillery tactics, at a salary of $1,200 per year, plus quarters. He accepted, turned his back on the United States Army, and resigned his commission. Jackson was already teaching at VMI by the time he was officially discharged in February 1852.

CHAPTER 5

Professor

JACKSON'S PLUNGE INTO OBSCURITY WAS PERHAPS THE BEST THING that could have happened to him. Following the Mexican War, the United States Army was reduced to only 16,000 men, and most officers were frozen in rank. Those who remained faced a difficult decade, as promotion became a waiting game with no regard to merit or service, simply a matter of being on the rolls when a slot opened up. Their duty stations were the 79 forts that formed the dusty necklace along the western frontier, where they fought boredom as much as they fought Indians.

There is no indication that Jackson regretted leaving the army or becoming tangled up in the problem in Florida. Moving to the sidelines harmed him not at all. When he did return to active military service almost a decade later, he would not be rejoining the U.S. Army anyway, and no one in the Confederacy cared a whit about a contretemps involving some unknown captain in the desolation of the Everglades.

In fact, upon accepting the VMI position, he jumped past many of his friends in rank, since professors were automatically awarded the full title of major. The position carried no formal standing beyond the walls of VMI, not even in the Virginia militia, but it was an important building block all the same.

+≡≡≡+

To train the VMI cadets in the use of artillery, Jackson had a battery of six harmless cannons and two howitzers. Since no horses were provided to pull the gun carriages, he had the cadets step into the harnesses and do the hauling. For an experienced artillery officer with actual combat time and a mastery of theory, the field practice was simple. He told the men what to do, and they did it, learning what they needed to know from the repetitious and strenuous drill. Everything on the field had to operate according to Jackson's smooth internal clock, and his reputation for punctuality found confirmation in the mock battle lessons. Move, set up, load, aim, and fire. Again.

Classrooms proved much more difficult. His awkwardness as a speaker and a basic shyness with strangers led him to boringly recite the lesson of the day, as if he were a breathing textbook. To protect his eyes, he avoided reading in artificial light. At night, he would sit straight up in his chair, staring at a wall in total silence while his busy mind shuffled the next day's lecture into proper order. For this unusual man who was to become a famous tactician, those daily, silent mental gymnastics would pay battlefield dividends, for no matter what hell was breaking out around him, Jackson could focus and think through a problem, step by step, to reach a conclusion totally unseen by others.

For his students, the machinelike result of his private planning was a horror. There were no variations to clarify a topic in Major Jackson's technical lectures on mathematics and optics and astronomy and science, no apparent understanding that a struggling cadet needed extra help, and no room at all for error—just the austere and hard-of-hearing professor standing or sitting rigidly straight at the front of the class, droning on in his high-pitched voice about some of the most difficult subjects a student could face. If asked to clarify something, he went all the way back to the beginning of that lesson and repeated what he had just said, word for word. Some cadets called him Tom Fool, one threatened to kill him, and even the VMI superintendent would later admit that Jackson "was no teacher." [1]

But the position spelled comfortable routine, and he fell in love with VMI, the town of Lexington, and the surrounding Blue Ridge Mountains. During this particularly tranquil period, Jackson completed the religious metamorphosis that would rule his remaining years. He joined the Lexington Presbyterian Church, the largest in town, in November of 1851 and wholeheartedly embraced its strict Calvinist teachings, including the principle of predestination, the idea that everything that happens has been ordained by God. He was a truly pious man who prayed frequently, worked for the church, studied his Bible daily, and discovered in its words the answers to everything, even why God favored slavery. His beliefs were no longer cluttered by his questioning spirit.

Jackson would frequently invoke the name of God and the values of Christianity even in the most personal conversations. Not only did he refuse to write or even read a letter on Sunday, he wanted to have mail deliveries halted entirely on the Sabbath. He did not impose his beliefs on outsiders, although he did bombard his sister Laura with missives about the path to redeeming glory. Instead of becoming a proselytizing missionary, he set out to perfect himself in the eyes of his God.

Jackson taught Sunday school (and even established one for slaves), became a deacon in the church, performed good works, went to prayer meetings, attended services twice on Sundays (sometimes falling asleep), and gave 10 percent of his earnings to the church. Prayer became so automatic, so much a part of him, that he would not even taste a glass of water without first giving a small prayer. Religion became an integral part of who he was, occupying almost every waking moment. Throughout the Civil War, he would to speak to God much more than he would talk to any man.

＋＞＝＜＋

While in Lexington, he was married twice, both times to daughters of presidents of nearby colleges. His first wife was a pretty girl named Elinor Junkins, an energetic daughter of the austere Presbyterian Reverend Doctor George Junkins, president of Washington College. A year younger than Jackson, she married him in 1853, and her sister accompanied them on the honeymoon. But a little more than a year later, she died delivering a still-born infant girl. Although the marriage was precious to him, Jackson controlled himself. He did not weep in public, and some black crepe around his sword handle and on his cap were the only outward signs of what must have been internal agony.

His second marriage came three years later, on July 16, 1857, to the vivacious Anna Morrison, one of the ten children of another Presbyterian minister, the Reverend Doctor Robert Hall Morrison, a former president of Davidson College. The child Anna bore him the next year, a daughter named Mary, died from disease a month after birth, and Jackson took comfort in the belief that she had entered Paradise.

Despite the unfortunate losses of his children and first wife, the marriages opened a rare window to a place of comfort in which the stern Major Jackson could lay aside his formal public self and enjoy a private life. There was a tenderness and kindness to the man, but he kept them tightly under wraps, revealing them only in the private sanctuary of his home. The professor, whom many cadets thought aloof and totally unfeeling, exhibited sheer playfulness with his wife, scaring her from behind doors, dancing the polka, and sweeping her into his arms. "We rarely ever met alone without caresses & endearing epithets," Anna would write.[2] But even at home, he did not take things easy. Each day began promptly at six o'clock with an earnest prayer on his knees, and then a cold water bath, no matter what the weather. His diets were spare, and he continued to pursued "water cures" for his health.

+═══◄+

The final important piece of the complex puzzle that was Thomas Jackson slid into place during the VMI years. He may have resigned from the army, but he did not forsake a military life. Rather, he embraced it on an intellectual level and enjoyed the luxuries of ample time, a cultured community, and access to books shops and college libraries, all of which helped him to master the craft and art of soldiering. Jackson the artilleryman had tasted combat and knew what it was like. Now Jackson the professor became an ardent student of the history of warfare and the tactics of the great fighters of the past, adding a number of military histories to his private library. It was not a matter of preparing himself for a specific conflict, but a logical step toward total understanding of his profession. As in all things, he attacked it with a dedicated ferociousness, and through his immense power of concentration, he absorbed history's great battles.

In 1856, between his two marriages, Jackson set off for a European tour. In typical fashion, he made every minute count, from his July departure until his October return to VMI. It was more of an intellectual assault than a merry sightseeing tour, and it became one of the favorite episodes of his life. He would caution people not to ask about his trip unless they were ready for a long dissertation.

The cities and towns of England, France, Belgium, Germany, Switzerland, and Italy unrolled before him in all their historic grandeur. He was deeply stirred by the art in Florence, where beautiful stone statues could be seen virtually everywhere and dozens of masterful portraits of the Madonna and her Sacred Child had been painted. Bookshops were places where printed treasures could be uncovered. Continental cuisine held no appeal, but the culture and history captivated him. Although it was no military tour, he did visit Waterloo, where he took a look at the famed battlefield and determined that Napoleon Bonaparte had attacked along the wrong axis.

+⫘+

His life during the VMI period was characterized by the unflinching determination branded on his character for all to see. As the years passed, he actually mellowed somewhat in dealing with his students, and after getting to know him, they similarly eased up on the criticism of his stern methods and even began to admire him.

That was an important milestone, for VMI was the West Point of the South. Many of the men who went on to lead the Confederate forces knew Stonewall Jackson before they ever set foot on a battlefield, for they had been his students. He had personally groomed a generation of future officers who, having seen his trademark willpower at work, believed that he would do exactly whatever he set out to do in war just as he did on campus.

His gritty spirit would galvanize an entire army, as the drums of secession began to beat and Jackson's comfortable, quiet VMI years came to a close. Battles were just over the horizon, and Thomas Jackson, holding the honorary rank of major but serving in no man's army, was about to go to war. He was ready.

CHAPTER 6

War

THE NATION STAGGERED BENEATH THE WEIGHT OF THE SLAVERY question. Bloody violence flared in Kansas. In Washington, Congressman Preston Brooks of South Carolina beat Massachusetts Senator Charles Sumner about the head with a gutta-percha cane. The U.S. Supreme Court ruled against Dred Scott, deciding that just because a slave lived in a free territory that did not make him free, and it later ruled that Congress could not prohibit slavery in the new territories. The anti-slavery book *Uncle Tom's Cabin* was on its way to becoming a classic.

Down in quiet Lexington, Major Jackson at VMI still hoped the states could work through their problems by peaceful means. A slave-owner himself, Jackson would soon see the chasm growing ever wider and realize the futility of those hopes.

The fanatical John Brown came out of Kansas determined to ignite a slave insurrection and create a nation of free black settlers in the Appalachian Mountains. His first goal was to seize the weapons at the Federal Arsenal in

Harper's Ferry, Virginia, less than 50 miles northwest of Washington. Leading a little gang of about 20 men, including several of his sons, Brown attacked on the night of October 16, 1859, but local residents and guards drove the raiders to shelter in a brick firehouse. President James Buchanan assigned Lieutenant Colonel Robert E. Lee of the U.S. Cavalry to lead some 90 Marines to Harper's Ferry and deal with the situation. Lee's dapper aide, First Lieutenant J. E. B. Stuart, banged on the firehouse door and demanded surrender, but Brown stalled. When Stuart waved his hat, the Marines charged, and it was all over in three minutes. Brown was taken prisoner and sentenced to be hanged for murder, treason, and conspiracy.

The Northern press and pro-Abolitionist forces lionized him as a champion of freedom, and the governor of Virginia, worried about a possible attempt to free Brown, summoned troops to protect the city. In addition to the militiamen, 86 cadets from VMI were also dispatched, with an artillery contingent under the command of Major Jackson. On the warm Friday morning of December 2 in Harper's Ferry, the troops formed a hollow square around a gallows and John Brown was brought forward in a wagon that also carried his oak coffin. As he dropped through the trapdoor, Jackson said a small prayer for the man's salvation. "I hope that he was prepared to die, but I am doubtful," Jackson wrote in a precise description of the event to Anna. "He refused to have a minister with him." [1]

Tension between North and South worsened over questions about the rights of individual states within the Union. As 1860 began, Jackson was quite concerned about the future, and the States' Rights issue gnawed at him. "If after we have done all we can. . . . there shall be a determination on the part of the Free States to deprive us of our rights. . . . I am in favor of secession," he wrote to his sister Laura in February.

The Democratic Presidential Convention that summer ended in uproar when the pro-slavery candidate, John C. Breckenridge of Kentucky, walked out, dividing the party and opening the way for Republican Abraham Lincoln to be elected president. South Carolina voted in December to secede, but Jackson still clung to a fading hope that the problems could be resolved without fighting. "I am strong for the Union at present, and if things become no worse I hope to continue so," he wrote to Laura.

Then Florida, Alabama, Georgia, Mississippi, and Louisiana also chose to leave the Union, and his allegiance waned. "I am in favor of making a thorough trial for peace, and if we fail in this, and the state is invaded, to defend it with a terrific resistance," he wrote to his young nephew, Thomas Arnold. [2]

When Texas seceded, 7 of the existing 34 states had bolted, and another 4 were expected to leave the Union—almost a third of the entire country—and even more were wavering.

Virginia and other upper-tier border states were still in the Union, although very tenuously, but they would not remain idle should the Federal government act against the states that had seceded. Other unlikely areas such as Oregon, California, and New Jersey began talking about pulling out of the Federal compact for various reasons. Something had to be done if the Union was to survive.

⊢══⊣

With time drawing short, former and current officers of the United States Army were forced to choose sides, knowing that it might eventually be up to them to decide the issues with dreadful finality. William Tecumseh Sherman resigned as superintendent of the college that would one day become the Louisiana State University, and moved to the North. Likewise, the superintendent of West Point, a Louisiana Creole named P.T. Beauregard, left that position after only five days in office and headed to the South, where he became the first brigadier general in the Confederate Army.

Jackson made his choice. He would defend Virginia. Laura, a staunch Unionist, was horrified at her brother's decision. Most VMI cadets strongly favored secession, but when Jackson found a secessionist flag flapping atop a barracks one morning, he promptly ordered it removed.

The end came before dawn on April 12, 1861, when General Beauregard's cannoneers opened a bombardment of Fort Sumter in the harbor of Charleston, and the bright red streaks of burning fuses on the artillery shells arced across South Carolina's coastal sky. Two days later, the Union garrison surrendered and was allowed to leave. Only one soldier had been killed, a Union trooper who died in an accident after the fighting was over.

The following day, the people of Lexington saw the growing strain firsthand. A downtown flag-raising incident escalated until VMI cadets squared off against a militia unit, both sides gripping muskets. Major Jackson told the boys to be patient, saying, "The time for war has not yet come yet, but it will come and that soon, and when it does come, my advice is to draw your swords and throw away the scabbard!"

+≻⚫≺+

President Lincoln called for 70,000 volunteers to join the armed forces of the United States to suppress the rebellion, but only for three-month enlistments—barely time to get them assembled and armed, much less trained—a decision that would have a serious impact on coming events. The presidential decree meant invasion, and it pushed Virginia to secede, followed by Arkansas, Tennessee, and North Carolina.

Virginia needed an army fast. Although one of the last states to secede, simple geography meant she would be one of the first to be invaded, for only the Potomac River separated the commonwealth from Washington, D.C.

Virginia adopted its secession ordinance only five days after Fort Sumter was fired upon, and VMI offered the services of a company of cadets. From all around the Old Dominion, militiamen, college students, the horseback-trained sons of the aristocracy, the strong boys of the farmers, and the bright kids of the merchants laid aside their work and went to the recruiting centers to volunteer for the army. The VMI cadets could help train them.

The commonwealth also drew in a proven hero, Colonel Robert E. Lee, the son of Revolutionary War cavalryman Henry "Light Horse Harry" Lee, and a cousin of Richard Henry Lee of the Continental Congress. His wife was a great-granddaughter of Martha Washington, and they lived in the white-columned Arlington House overlooking Washington. Second in his class at West Point in 1829, he carved a brilliant war record in Mexico, earning three brevet promotions, and then served as superintendent of West Point before commanding a cavalry regiment on the western frontier for three years. As the Civil War stumbled to a start, Lee was promoted to full colonel in the 1st Cavalry, then was offered command of the U.S. Army. Although he favored neither slavery nor secession, Robert E. Lee declined. He would fight for Virginia, and Richmond appointed him to be a major general.

+≻⚫≺+

On Sunday morning, April 21, Major Thomas Jackson did not attend church, for orders had come from Richmond summoning a large contingent of fully armed and supplied VMI cadets, and Jackson was placed in charge. After packing, reading from the fifth chapter of Second Corinthians in his Bible, and praying with his wife, he supervised final details for the movement in a manner so unhurried that it tried the patience of the eager cadets. The orders said to move out at one o'clock, and the punctilious Jackson waited until the gong sounded the hour before sending them on the march. The 176 cadets and 8 officers made good time by marching, stagecoach, and train, and arrived in Richmond the following evening.

The cadets, trained in drill and military discipline, were quickly dispersed to be drill sergeants for the volunteers and militiamen pouring into "Camp Lee," established on the broad fields west of Richmond. Jackson, with no real job left to do, was assigned topographical map duties. Holding the honorary rank of major at VMI, he was now given the rank of major in the engineers of the Virginia Militia, which was about to be dismantled. He had so much time on his hands that he personally taught a lost young soldier how to be a sentry. Chafing for a new assignment, he busied himself writing letters, contacting old friends, and working among his political allies.

<hr/>

A top priority for the military and political planners, as it had been for John Brown, was to seize Harper's Ferry, where 10,000 guns were made every year at the Federal Arsenal, and some 17,000 finished muskets were stored along with enormous quantities of ammunition. Brown had only wanted the weapons, but the town at the junction of the Potomac and Shenandoah Rivers also had strategic importance as a transportation and communications hub. Virginia was on one side of the Potomac and neutral Maryland was on the other, and the Baltimore & Ohio Railroad, a major east-west link for Washington, crossed a Potomac bridge there, with telegraph lines laced beside the tracks.

Harper's Ferry had become the northeastern point of the Confederacy, and it was defended by only 45 U.S. Army soldiers under the command of First Lieutenant Roger Jones, who happened to be a cousin of Robert E. Lee. Jones notified his superiors that the place could not be held without thousands of reinforcements, but the Federal government did not have thousands to send. Even if more troops did arrive, they still would be jammed into a valley trapped at the confluence of two big rivers and surrounded by a triangle of high hills. Whoever controlled those hills controlled the village. As both sides would find out, seldom has such an important military position been so condemned by its location.

Lieutenant Jones waited until the Confederate troops were less than a mile from town, then set the armory and the riverside storehouses to the torch and led his handful of men across the Potomac to safety. The fire became an inferno, but not everything was destroyed. The metal workings of thousands of weapons and much of the machinery survived the flames, and many guns had been stashed away by locals. Everything that could be scavenged militarily was sent away to safer locations, and most of the residents packed up and left.

The town was now in possession of the South, occupied by some 2,500 militiamen and volunteers led by officers who were not trained military men but hometown favorites and political appointees. The crowd of commanders included one major general, three brigadiers, and flocks of preening underlings and staff members.

Naming of a real commander fell to the Executive War Council in Richmond at about the same time that Jackson's influential friends were protesting the waste of such a tested officer who was a known quantity on a battlefield. Why was he tethered to a map room while less qualified men were being given rank and important assignments?

"Who is this Major Jackson, that we are asked to commit him to so responsible a post?" demanded a member of the Secession Convention.

A friend from the western mountains answered, "He is one, who, if you order him to hold a post, will never leave it alive to be occupied by the enemy." [3]

With the consent of the governor, Jackson was promoted to colonel in the Virginia Volunteers and assigned command of the unruly mob at Harper's Ferry.

Jackson gave thanks to God and left Richmond immediately, with four VMI comrades who were to be his staff and drill instructors. Feeling as though a dream had come true, he wrote his wife that he had been given an independent command and "the post which I prefer above all others." [4]

It was time for seasoned professionals to take over, and the gold braid generals and their glittering staff members of the various state militias were dismissed. On April 29, the silent, newly minted colonel and his few comrades came clattering into Harper's Ferry aboard a train that rolled on wooden rails. Instead of a beautiful officer's coat, Jackson arrived wearing the same drab blue tunic he had worn every day at VMI, where only two weeks before he had been teaching in a classroom. A small campaign cap tilted low on his forehead shaded his excited eyes.

CHAPTER 7

Command

NOW IT BEGAN. ALL OF THE ELEMENTS THAT JACKSON HAD GATH-ered throughout his life, pebbles of knowledge and polished stones of experi-ence, were coming into play. This was where he belonged, in uniform and with an independence of command that allowed him to do as he wished. Harper's Ferry reeled as if a hurricane had moved through, but instead of sowing destruction, he restored order and created a sense of purpose.

"The presence of a master mind was visible in the changed condition of the camp. Perfect order reigned everywhere," wrote the amazed artillery Captain John Imboden upon returning to camp after having been away when Jackson arrived.

Instruction in the details of military duties occupied Jackson's whole time. He urged the officers to call upon him for information about even the minutest details of duty, often remarking that it was no discredit to a civilian to be ignorant of military matters. He was a rigid disciplinarian, and yet as gentle and kind as a woman. He was the easiest man in our army to get along with pleasantly so long as one did his duty, but as inexorable as fate in exacting the performance of it; yet he would overlook serious faults if he saw they were the result of ignorance, and would instruct the offender in a kindly way. He was as courteous to the humblest private who sought an interview for any purpose as to the highest officer in his command. He despised superciliousness and self-assertion, and nothing angered him so quickly as to see an officer wound the feelings of those under him by irony or sarcasm. [1]

Jackson, having been in Harper's Ferry for the execution of John Brown, was quite aware that the surrounding hills made a secure defense impossible. Complicating matters was that one of the strategic high points was in Maryland, which the South hoped to lure into the Confederacy and did not want to antagonize by occupying its "neutral" territory.

Several thousand independent-minded militiamen and new volunteers had to be trained from scratch. Young gentlemen who arrived with personal slaves and clean linen learned to their discomfort that they were now of the same status as youngsters in homespun clothing and hats made from animal skins. Jackson saw only opportunity, a chance to organize and train them as he felt best. He knew that the paramount way to keep them alive, and fighting, was to toughen them up from the start, and his training regimen was intentionally harsh.

The days began before dawn and went for 17 hours, until the men were allowed to collapse into their bedrolls at night. They marched at least seven hours every single day, rain or shine, and if anyone tried to dodge work by going to see the doctor, the general would be watching.

Twenty-mile marches with pack and musket to improve endurance were not abnormal, and when the men were not marching, they were wielding picks and shovels to build a dozen miles of fortifications. Jackson personally inspected every outlying position after sending orders ahead that he was not to be saluted. Guards roamed the perimeters all day and night.

Hundreds of new men, units from Alabama and Kentucky, as well as more Virginians, arrived daily and were absorbed into his training program. He organized them into companies, and then sorted the companies into regiments. Jackson had been educating young men for the past ten years and knew how to wring from them what he needed. He was teaching boys to become soldiers, molding men to become officers—time was short and he intended to defend the indefensible Harper's Ferry to the last man, if need be.

Above all, he taught them discipline—that orders must be followed. Obedience was everything. A story that circulated among the troops at VMI illustrates just how seriously he took orders himself. Instructed to report to the superintendent's office, Jackson took a seat in the hallway, unseen, and the superintendent forgot the appointment and left by another door. When he arrived the next morning, Jackson was still patiently waiting in the hall, where he had remained all night. He had taken the appointment to be a direct order, and would never leave a duty station until properly relieved.

His reputation for quirkiness had followed him to Harper's Ferry, but so did the belief that Colonel Jackson was religious, honest, brave, totally confident, determined, qualified, and completely a man of his word. Confidence grew that the colonel could mold this raw force into a superb fighting unit. They would respond to the call for strong discipline and would do what they were told, even when bullets were zipping around their ears.

Jackson was itching for offensive warfare, not an immobile defensive position, and in defiance of Richmond's warnings, he moved 500 men on the Maryland Heights. Lee mildly upbraided him for that unapproved movement.

<hr />

His independent command lasted less than a month, as the War Department soon expanded and, on May 15, 1861, appointed Major General Joseph E. Johnston to take charge of the all Southern forces in the area. Colonel Jackson politely informed the major general that he had received no written orders to turn over his command, and therefore declined to do so until such instructions came from Richmond. The two senior officers settled their differences amicably when Johnston produced a letter from Lee from which Jackson could infer that the transfer of command was legal.

It was another signal that Jackson obeyed orders to the letter, and expected everyone else, both the generals above him and the privates below, to do the same.

The man he faced down without hesitation was a legend. Joe Johnston in that year was 54 years old, small and trim with a gray goatee. Another native Virginian, he had been a West Point classmate of Lee and had fought and been wounded in the Indian wars. In Mexico, he was wounded five more times and awarded several promotions before going on to fight in California, Kansas, and Utah.

When the Civil War began, Johnston was a brigadier general and the quartermaster general of the U.S. Army, the highest ranking officer to resign and cross over into the Confederacy. During the Civil War, he would again be seriously wounded and again recover. His death would not come until 30 years later, after he caught pneumonia while serving as a pallbearer in the funeral of his old enemy, Union General William Tecumseh Sherman, to whom he had surrendered at the end of the war.

General Johnston found more than 7,000 men under his banner and an army growing larger by the day, so he banded the regiments together in order to form three brigades. In a fateful decision, he put all of the Virginians into a single unit, the 1st Brigade, and awarded its command to Colonel Jackson.

Most of the brigade members hailed from the long, narrow Shenandoah Valley, a fertile corridor that started at busy towns such as Winchester, Martinsburg, and Harper's Ferry in the northeast and slid hundreds of miles to the southwest into rural and isolated communities such as Wytheville, Abington, and Bristol Station. The rugged Alleghenies defined the northern edge, and the Blue Ridge Mountains bordered the south. Being grouped together with men they had known all of their lives lent a family reunion atmosphere to what they were doing, and constantly reminded them that when the war started, it would be in the places they knew best amidst the people they loved most.

The brigade mushroomed into 2,600 men, who were distributed among the 2nd, the 4th, the 5th, the 27th, and the 33rd Virginia infantry regiments and supported by artillery components drawn from Jackson's own area, Lexington, the county seat of Rockbridge County. The gunners of the Rockbridge Artillery were educated young men led by a crusty middle-aged

Episcopal minister and West Pointer, the Reverend William Nelson Pendleton. Their four guns were named after the first books of the New Testament: Matthew, Mark, Luke, and John. The nuggets of two regiments of horsemen were established under a pair of daring officers who would rank among the war's most outstanding cavalry leaders, Jeb Stuart and Turner Ashby. The Shenandoah boys of the 1st Brigade were a rowdy brotherhood unified by a stern father figure, the eccentric but trusted Colonel Jackson, who pushed them to their limits, and then beyond, into legend.

"This organization made an impact on history few units can match," wrote historian James Robertson. "It has been likened to the Macedonian Phalanx of Alexander, the Tenth Legion of Caesar, the Paladines of Charlemagne, the Ironsides of Cromwell, and the Old Guard of Napoleon. . . . They were rough fighters [who] came to the conviction that they could defeat any given number of Yankees at any time—a conviction amply justified by their war record." [2]

When in the saddle, Jackson, who never rode well, oversaw the brigade operations while wobbling unsteadily upon a small, ungainly brown horse that he had purchased for his wife at Harper's Ferry. He had named the animal "Fancy," but his men called it "Little Sorrel" because of its size and color. Just like its owner's, its looks were deceiving, for Little Sorrel would stand rock solid in a hail of gunfire, and while it might not win a race or a beauty contest when paired against some thoroughbred stallion, Little Sorrel could *walk* any horse into the ground, trudging mile after mile after mile.

<hr />

The first real fight came along the Ohio River, where the young, cocky, and brilliant George McClellan, the brightest light in Jackson's West Point class of 1846, became the Union's first hero. At 34, McClellan had already enjoyed successful military and business careers before returning to uniform on being made a major general in the Union Army. Everyone, including McClellan himself, believed he was destined for glory. He was given responsibility for the zone north of the Alleghenies. The large section of Virginia behind that mountain range, some two-fifths of the state, wanted nothing to do with secession, and was about to counter-secede from its rebel motherland when a Confederate force of 4,000 men went to compel it to remain in the fold.

McClellan led 8,000 men against these Confederates, declaring as soon as he crossed the Ohio River, "Soldiers! I have heard that there was danger here. I have come to place myself at your head and to share it with you."[3] A series of tough skirmishes pushed back the Confederates, and McClellan became a national hero. Two years later, the area would join the Union as West Virginia, the thirty-fifth state.

Yankee pride over that victory dimmed when far to the south at Big Bethel, near the tip of the Virginia peninsula, a Federal general decided to chase off some Rebel units by attacking at night through a swamp. The waiting Southerners felt as if they were shooting rabbits, so easy was it to pick off the enemy troops. Seventy-six dead and wounded Union soldiers were the price of the general's folly.

The loss at Big Bethel rattled Washington, where patriotic citizens were demanding that the Union Army sweep over the Confederates and end the war quickly. General-in-Chief Winfield Scott advocated a slow-but-sure plan to constrict the South's supply points while building and training an army large enough to win a decisive victory. The strategy was sound, but it would take years to work, and the political forces were impatiently crying, "Forward to Richmond!" President Lincoln also recognized that the 90-day terms of those who answered his call for volunteers were rapidly expiring. He argued to Scott that because the Southern armies were also green and untrained, the Union should strike quickly. The result was a plan to move on Richmond with the forces already at hand.

The first huge battle of the Civil War was brewing, and Colonel Thomas Jackson and his tough 1st Brigade would be right in the middle of it.

＋➤━➤╋

Reaching the same conclusion as every other professional military man who ever set foot in Harper's Ferry, General Joe Johnston saw that the place could not be held against a determined enemy. He received permission from Lee to abandon the position, and over the next two weeks, he left the heights, destroyed the public buildings and the long metal bridge across the Potomac, and marched his Confederate troops out of the important little town that everyone wanted to have but none could afford to keep.

He moved back some 30 miles to the southwest, to the Winchester area at the mouth of the Shenandoah, a major crossroads city with access to the only railroad heading into northern Virginia.

By June 19, Jackson had appeared in Martinsburg, ten miles almost due north of Winchester, to raid the huge depot of the Baltimore & Ohio Railroad and destroy everything he could not remove. Throughout the war, Jackson would haul in enormous quantities of railroad booty for the South, from tools to track and even heavy engines pulled over dirt roads by teams of harnessed horses. This mission, however, was only about destruction, and his men set huge fires that consumed buildings, 42 locomotives, and more than 300 rolling cars. The devastation was so great that Jackson lamented to his wife: "It was your husband who did so much mischief at Martinsburg. To destroy so many fine locomotives, cars and railroad property was sad work, but I had my orders, and it was my duty to obey. If the cost of the property could only have been expended in disseminating the gospel of the Prince of Peace, how much good might have been expected!"[4]

A huge Union force raced toward Winchester from the north, and General Johnston drew a defensive line around the town of Bunker Hill, a few miles away.

Commanding the oncoming Union army was Major General Robert Patterson, from County Tyrone, Ireland, which his family fled after an Irish uprising against the British crown. He had been a young infantry lieutenant in the War of 1812 and a major general in Mexico, where he was an effective field commander and also a member of General Scott's staff. After that war, Patterson had success in politics and business, acquiring financial holdings that included a sugar plantation in Louisiana and 30 cotton mills in Pennsylvania. Called back into uniform for the crisis, once again as a major general, he was put in charge of a sprawling "military department" that included troops from Pennsylvania, Delaware, Maryland, and the District of Columbia. He seemed ideal for the post.

But Patterson was by then 69 years of age, and his superior officer in Washington, General-in-Chief Scott, was even older, and communications between the two old men were often garbled and misunderstood.

Scott was sending a large force into northern Virginia to hit the Confederates at a strategic communications hub called Manassas Junction. He told Patterson to keep General Johnston's Rebel troops busy up around Winchester. With bands playing brightly, Patterson crossed the Potomac on July 2 and invaded Virginia with about 15,000 men and unclear orders.

Confederate cavalry scouts alerted Johnston, who had about 9,000 men. Jackson and his 1st Brigade were among them, brimming with confidence and spoiling for a fight.

CHAPTER 8

General

JACKSON DID NOT LEARN THAT THE NORTHERN TROOPS WERE coming toward him until they were just five miles away, masses of men in blue uniforms in long columns snaking across the rolling fields and through the woods. He was ordered to respond to the threat without igniting an all-out engagement, and he hastened forward with less than 500 men from his 5th Virginia Regiment and a single cannon from the Rockbridge Artillery. The opposing sides found each other near a church called Falling Waters.

The Virginians drove back the outer skirmishers, but Union regiments soon began to arrive, one after another. Federal cavalry came trotting up the crowded road, right into range of the gun commanded by the Reverend Pendleton, who turned his face to heaven and hollered, "May the Lord have mercy on their wicked souls! Fire!"[1] His cannon roared and the ball slammed into the men and horses, clearing the road.

Jackson was sitting on a big rock near the artillery piece and writing a dispatch to General Johnston when a Federal ball fired in response crashed into a nearby white oak tree and showered him with dirt, bark, and splinters. He impatiently brushed away the debris, finished his note and handed it to a courier. In a sudden move to catch the Union off-balance, Jackson gave Jeb Stuart permission to take his hard-riding cavalrymen around the Federal right flank, and the Rebel troopers snatched two enemy officers and 47 soldiers as prisoners.

When Jackson estimated that the numbers of Union troops outnumbered his own men about four-to-one, he began a slow, methodical retreat back to the main Confederate lines, blocking the Federals each time they moved too close. The tactic masked the true size of his inferior force and allowed him enough time even to bring back his baggage and supply wagons. The Reverend Pendleton's lone cannon was fired only eight times during the textbook delaying action.

Patterson was so thoroughly fooled by Jackson that he claimed a victory, and announced that he had defeated a Rebel force that he estimated at about 3,500 men. Then, with the Rebels only a dozen miles away, he stopped in his tracks. His orders were to pin them down, and he believed that he knew exactly where they were.

The following day, on July 3, a personal letter from Lee arrived for Colonel Jackson. "My dear general, I have the pleasure of sending you a commission of brigadier-general in the Provisional Army, and to feel that you merit it," wrote Lee. "May your advancement increase your usefulness to the State."[2]

Jackson had been lobbying for the promotion out of concern that he was only a colonel, and since a brigade normally was commanded by a brigadier general, someone new might be appointed to take over his brigade. He also was hoping a promotion would accompany the assignment to defend his home area in southwestern Virginia. The single star of a brigadier general stitched on the shoulders of his old VMI coat solved the first problem, but his home territory would have to get along without him.

"I have had all that I ought to desire in the line of promotion. I should be very ungrateful if I were not contented, and exceedingly thankful to our kind Heavenly father," Jackson wrote to his wife. [3]

His illnesses, real or imagined, seemed to respond to the medicine of action, just as they had in Mexico. Two weeks after the Falling Waters affair, he wrote Anna that he had eaten cornbread and slept out in the camp, "and generally found that it agreed with me well, except when it rained, and even then it was but slightly objectionable. I find that sleeping in the open air, with no covering but my blankets and the blue sky for a canopy, is more refreshing than sleeping in a room."[4] The more he was deprived of creature comforts, the better Jackson seemed to be.

Thousands of Union soldiers had settled in around Martinsburg and celebrated Independence Day on July 4. The Southern troops facing them did not, for the holiday marked the founding of a nation not their own.

⊹══⊱

The Blue Ridge Mountains along the ragged southern edge of the Shenandoah Valley are penetrated by gaps that proved strategically important, passes and valleys that allowed access and egress. Prior to the war, a group of speculators had built a small railroad through one of those breeches in order to connect the productive farmlands of the Valley with the markets and ports along the coast. The rail line ran east from Strasburg, deep in the valley, snaking through the Manassas Gap and linking up with Orange and Alexandria Railroad at Manassas Junction. It was appropriately called the Manassas Gap Railroad, and in the summer of 1861, the little line assumed huge importance, for it connected the two Confederate armies that were located about one hundred miles apart.

In Washington, political pressure for action had reached a breaking point, and Brigadier General Irwin McDowell was chosen to command the dash to Richmond. The Ohio native was very popular, but had never led troops in battle, not even in Mexico. He possessed an agile mind but could not remember names and did not listen closely. While he abstained from drinking alcohol, he devoured immense amounts of food, once eating a whole watermelon for dessert.

When the war began and he was given the daunting task of building the largest army ever put together in America, he complained that the bumbling volunteers and the supply efforts he found in an inefficient War Department needed a lot of work. He protested that this huge new organization, called the Army of Northern Virginia, was not ready to fight, but Lincoln responded by insisting that neither were the Southern troops. At two o'clock in the afternoon of July 16, McDowell put 30,000 men on the road to Manassas Junction, keeping another 10,000 ready in reserve.

The Confederate commander awaiting him was his old friend and West Point classmate General Pierre Gustave Toutant-Beauregard, who had become extremely popular in the South after commanding the attack on Fort Sumter. Taking Sumter had been easy, but now Beauregard, with only about 18,000 men, had to defend the heart of the Old Dominion against a numerically superior force. Richmond sent new troops as they became available, but he constantly pleaded for more.

As the Union threat increased, Beauregard begged Richmond to start shifting the General Johnston's troops down from Winchester, but he was refused. The government did not relent until July 17, after the Union horde had already surged forward; by then, time had run out. Reading the news that his reinforcements were on the way, Beauregard furiously threw the message into the dirt, muttering that it was too late. The enemy would reach him before Johnston's units could arrive.

+———=+

Early in the summer, Federal forces had snatched the Arlington and Alexandria areas just across the Potomac from the Capitol, but when they stepped off to venture deeper into the Virginia countryside, they were tripped up by their lack of discipline, training, and experience. The shaky advance fell apart on the very first afternoon, and General McDowell watched with disgust from beneath the brim of a bowl-shaped straw hat as the long columns repeatedly halted and moved for no discernable reasons, the men simply falling out of ranks when they wished to pick blackberries or fill their canteens with water.

In contrast to the hardened troops of Thomas Jackson, the Federal recruits could not handle the long march, covering only ten miles the first day in the searing heat and choking dust of the summer. Having gobbled all of the rations that were meant to last for the entire campaign, thousands of them resorted to stealing chickens and milk and shooting cows for the dinner pots as the schedule fell to pieces.

Tagging along with the army was a large contingent of merry civilians, including congressmen in carriages, squadrons of newspaper reporters, and women in gay summer frocks, all of whom had turned out to see the grand spectacle of battle. Music from regimental bands stirred their hearts.

While the Union advance stalled, the Confederates moved. In a total reversal of roles, Jeb Stuart's cavalry now pinned Patterson down by providing an annoying screen that kept the Union commander enthralled and idle near Winchester while Rebel regiments slipped away and headed for Manassas, on the other side of the mountains.

Jackson's road-trained brigade took off so fast they left their tents behind for others to gather. At one rest point, Jackson read aloud the orders from General Johnston: "Our gallant army under General Beauregard is now attacked by overwhelming numbers. The commanding general hopes that his troops will step out like men, and make a forced march to save the country." His brigade responded with energy and enthusiasm, and after a hard march, they waded across the cold, waist-deep water of the Shenandoah River just as night fell. Reaping the dividends of their harsh training, they kept going, incredibly, until about two o'clock the following morning, when Jackson let the exhausted soldiers sleep for a few hours. Legend has it that he kept watch himself. He had them marching again in the early morning darkness, and they reached the Manassas Gap Railroad about dawn. They piled onto the rolling stock and became the lead element of reinforcements heading to Manassas.

The following day, Brigadier General Thomas Jackson would move to the battlefield.

CHAPTER 9

Stonewall

THE SHEER MASS OF THE STUMBLING FEDERAL FORCE MADE BEAU-
regard abandon thoughts of attacking, and he deployed his 18,000 Confederate troops along a six-mile front behind the water barrier of Bull Run
Creek. With its steep and slippery banks, the meandering waterway could be
crossed only at a few places other than the Stone Bridge along the Warrenton
Turnpike. Beauregard anchored that defensible bridge, a bottleneck, with a
half-brigade and concentrated his strength at crossing points that stepped off
to the right of it.

The unexpected delays had thrown the Union Army off schedule by
three days, but with the distance between the two sides inexorably closing,
skirmishes began to break out as reconnaissance units tested the Southern
perimeter, particularly at Blackburn's Ford, where McDowell had wanted to
force a passage. For many, officers and enlisted men alike, it was an introduc-
tion to what gunfire and cannonballs could do to human flesh, and it was
more than enough for some of Lincoln's "ninety-day men." Their enlistments

had expired on June 15, and they wanted no part of what lay ahead. A New York artillery battery and a Pennsylvania infantry regiment turned around and marched back to Washington, leaving the field before the battle even started.

+≻←≺+

General McDowell abandoned the plan to plow through the center of what he realized was a strong Confederate defense line by the bridge and led his army on a massive flanking movement. They started before dawn on Sunday, July 21, with bright moonlight showing the way west and south out of Centreville. Thousands of marching feet moved through the dark valleys, across the hills, and along the roads. As morning broke, a Confederate private at the Stone Bridge saw clouds of dust rising to the sky, and then Federal artillery opened up, sending "shot and shell . . . screaming like lost spirits through the air."[1] The action at the bridge was only a feint, because McDowell had sent 10,000 other Union soldiers wheeling away north to go around the Confederate left flank.

It was eight thirty in the morning before the Confederates recognized that the artillery duels along the river fords directly before them had masked the crossing of two full Federal divisions at virtually undefended Sudley Ford, a mile and a half to the north. "Look out for your left. You are turned," came a shocking signal to the commander at the Stone Bridge. Union soldiers were moving over open ground only five paces apart as the Confederates hastened to shift forces to the threatened area, with panting infantrymen running and artillerymen putting the lash to the horses pulling the cannons. The morning air filled with the buzzing of musket balls, the explosions of cannon fire, and the screams of dying men and animals.

On a warm, sunny, and safe hillside about a mile away, a woman from Washington put her opera glasses to her eyes and exclaimed in delight to the other picnicking Sunday spectators, "That is splendid! Oh, my! Is not that first-rate? I guess we will be in Richmond this time tomorrow."[2] Even untrained observers could see that the Federals were winning.

What could not be seen was that the Confederate force was growing by the hour. Joe Johnston, who had completely fooled Patterson at Winchester, marched about two-thirds of his men to the Piedmont Station and loaded them onto the tiny railroad that fed into Manassas Junction 34 miles away. The hoot of steam whistles, the clang of couplings, and the smoke of busy locomotives would become part of the lore of Bull Run, for it marked one of the first times in warfare that railroad mobility was used to shift such a large number of troops. Instead of being idled in front of Patterson, Johnston's Rebels were rushing toward Bull Run, and fresh regiments would arrive throughout the battle.

General Thomas Jackson's 2,600 Virginians had been among the first to arrive on Saturday, and after disembarking had passed the time in a beautiful countryside dotted with pines near Blackburn's Ford and Mitchell's Ford on the Confederate right. Fresh graves told the story of the earlier skirmishing there. With another brigade in front of them along the river, the 1st Brigade had time to catch its breath.

For Jackson, the prospect of doing battle on a Sunday brought conflicting feelings. Doing almost anything other than going to church and praying was abhorrent to him on the Sabbath, but he welcomed the opportunity to get into the fight. He began Sunday, his wife's thirtieth birthday, at prayer on his knees in the early morning darkness, then roused his men at about three o'clock and had them make ready.

The apparel of the opposing armies had not yet been standardized; uniforms were so mixed that Jackson himself still wore his blue VMI tunic, while some of his men wore gray and others wore blue. Being able to tell friend from foe would be vital, so he ordered them to tie white strips about their hats for instant identification in the fog of battle.

He began receiving orders that had him jockeying segments of his command first in one way and then another, until the thunder on the distant left erased any doubt about the location of the real fighting. At about nine thirty in the morning, orders came to move to the area of the Stone Bridge, and Jackson put his hard-drilled soldiers at double-quick time, running through the rusty dust toward the sound of guns. Within 90 minutes, they were at the edge of the battle in a four-abreast column, but Jackson halted them before most of them even saw the enemy, and before the enemy spotted them.

They were on the eastern side of Henry House Hill, about a hundred yards from a weathered white farmhouse that gave the place its name. In it, Judith Henry, the 80-year-old matriarch, lay dying on her bed; during the coming battle she would be killed by cannon fire. The only other house on the plateau was owned by a free Negro. Some historians have questioned why Jackson did not immediately commit to the raging battle; the answer is that he recognized the strategic value of the geography.

The ridge was almost at a right angle to the northeastern end of the Stone Bridge, and the crest had been cleared of trees, as had the western slope, which dropped into a valley. Any attackers would have to cross bare, open ground that would quickly become a killing field. The Warrenton Turnpike, worn to a deep ditch by years of use, ran past the hill to a crossroads on the left, from which another road led up to Sudley Ford, where the Federal units were still crossing. With the bridge at one end and the crossroad at the other, whoever dominated the heights of Henry Hill would control the battle.

From a defensive perspective, Jackson saw that the thick groves of pine trees covering the reverse, or eastern, slope could also provide some protection for his troops.

The battle was already in full throat as he spread the 1st Brigade into position, and wounded men, running cowards, and disorganized soldiers drifted back through their lines. Jackson spurred Little Sorrel up the rise and looked through the rolling clouds of gun smoke to see that Union forces were taking control of everything northwest of the Warrenton Pike.

Beyond the turnpike was Matthews Hill, which was crawling with long lines of blue Federal infantrymen smashing against the wavering Confederate line. Approximately 3,000 Confederate troops who had been shifted to meet the enemy sweep had been mauled in the morning's fight. Union artillery pieces continued booming unmolested.

Jackson knew there would be little point in feeding his brigade piecemeal into such a battle when the enemy forces would be coming at them in a matter of minutes anyway. So instead of leaving the high ground, Jackson put it to work for him, building what would become the defensive cornerstone of the entire battle.

As an artillery expert, he aligned his five regiments along the reverse slope so the Union guns could not hit them with direct fire. Indeed, the Federal troops could not even *see* the Virginians. Jackson's line stretched from his 5th Regiment on the right to the 33rd Regiment on the left, both burrowed deeply into the thick pines and sturdy oaks. Jeb Stuart's cavalry supported the 33rd. The 500 yards between those groves were lined by the 4th, the

27th, and the 2nd Regiments, all behind and supporting artillery pieces that were also just below the protective crest. From there, they could load, roll up to the top, fire, and let the recoil shove them back down the slope.

Then Jackson had his men do something that would terrify any soldier—lie flat on the ground and passively endure a beating from the Northern artillery, which was already raging ruthlessly over them.

+≻═≺+

Both Generals Joe Johnston and Pierre Beauregard rode up to the new front at about noon. They were working together in order to avoid a potentially harmful disagreement on overall command. Johnston was the senior, but he allowed Beauregard, who knew the situation better, to continue guiding the fight, while Johnston kept shoveling in the reinforcements. In any case, there was little more they could do, for tactical command of the all-important center of the line had fallen to someone else: 37-year-old Brigadier General Thomas Jackson.

With his frightened infantrymen chewing dirt and praying as the musket balls flew overhead, Jackson rode easily aboard Little Sorrel in front of them, a picture of total calm. He turned his face toward the heavens as if expecting rain, though the only thing coming down was death and destruction. "All's well," he told his soldiers in soft words and with a mild smile. "All's well."[3]

But Jackson himself soon became one of the brigade's early casualties. While talking with another officer, the general held his left arm out with his hand straight up, one of his many peculiarities, and a musket ball hit his left hand, breaking his middle finger and lacerating his forefinger. He yanked his hand down in a flash of pain, wrapped a handkerchief around it, and resumed his study of the fight.

The battle surged to them at about two o'clock in the afternoon, and Jackson brought his men off the ground into a kneeling position. The Virginians were eager to engage, tired of just lying there while the Union cannonades pounded them. Bayonets were slammed onto the ends of the long rifles.

General Bernard Bee, with sword in hand, galloped up and told Jackson that his 4th Alabama Brigade had been broken on Mathews Hill and was falling back. Sweat drenched his long hair and his dark eyes flashed fiercely as he told his old West Point friend, "General, they are driving us!"

Jackson's blue eyes seemed lit by an inner fire. "Sir, we will give them the bayonet!" [4]

That was enough for Bee, who hurried back to his retreating brigade, which was streaming back past the Henry House with Union artillery on their heels. They wanted rest and safety, but Bee wanted them to turn and fight again. He pointed his sword toward the man on the small horse upon the hill and shouted, "Look, men, there is Jackson standing like a stone wall! Let us determine to die here, and we will conquer! Follow me!" He then plunged back into the fight, only to have his horse shot out from under him. As he stalked on foot among his troops, Bee was fatally shot. He is remembered in history not for his own exceptional personal valor, but for coining Jackson's famous nickname.

Then the storm broke on them all, but Jackson still would not rush into the fight. Still strong and intact, he intended for his brigade to provide a solid bulwark around which the units broken on Matthew's Hill could rally on his right, while Johnston's reinforcements expanded and strengthened his left, where masses of Union troops were pressing. The battle was about to take a momentous turn, and Jackson and his Virginia brigade were to be the pivot.

The two armies pounded each other with musket fire while artillery bursts shook the ground, and men fell all along the line. Neither side could gain a significant advantage, for although the North had a larger number of troops, the South had control of the slopes of Henry House Hill.

General McDowell threw four brigades into the attack, but they were so uncoordinated that they moved as separate regiments instead of a solid wave of attackers. On the left of Jackson's line, two Union artillery batteries with a total of 11 guns made the mistake of moving halfway up the slope in the hopes of bombarding the Confederate infantrymen there. In doing so, the gunners had put themselves outside their umbrella of infantry protection, prompting Jeb Stuart, who was waiting in the nearby woods, to attack, a move that earned a rare grin of approval from the watching Jackson. Stuart's troopers drew their pistols and sabers, dug in their spurs, and charged headlong into the colorful Zouaves from New York, slashing and shooting until the unit famed for its red pantaloons and white turbans broke and fled. The 33rd Virginia Regiment, looking from a distance much like Federal troops in their blue jackets, simultaneously ventured from the woods and confused the Union commanders, who let them get close enough to unleash murderous volleys at point-blank range on the critical artillery position. They captured one entire battery and drove off all but three guns of the second, tilting the balance of power on that side of the field. After a day of falling back, the Confederate successes buoyed hope along the line.

But the 33rd was ripped in turn and eventually driven back, suffering such heavy losses that one of its officers galloped over to Jackson and shouted, "General! The day is going against us!" Jackson, who wanted no such defeatism alarming his men, growled in response, "If you think so, sir, you had better not say anything about it."[5] On the far right, heavy fighting had erupted after fresh Union troops crossed Bull Run nearer the Stone Bridge, but there were no breakthroughs at either end.

McDowell, with a two-to-one advantage in troops, unleashed a powerful assault directly against the middle of the line, and more Union troops headed up the forbidding slope to take out the Confederate artillery, confidently calling, "On to Richmond!" They had not realized that the bulk of Jackson's force was concealed just behind the crest of the ridge.

Neither had many of Jackson's men, despite being pounded by Union artillery for more than two and one-half hours, actually laid eyes on an enemy soldier. Still, their general held them in check, telling them, "Reserve your fire until they come within fifty yards! Then fire and give them the bayonet! And when you charge, yell like furies."[6]

The fight ignited like an explosion when the Virginia regiments rose as one and met the oncoming Federal soldiers with a massive and unexpected volley of artillery and musket fire that decimated the Union troops and stopped the advance cold. A second and then a third charge were also met by impenetrable walls of Rebel fire. Union soldiers, who had held the advantage all day, finally broke, and at three thirty in the afternoon, Jackson unleashed his brigade in a vicious counter-attack. With the southern sunshine gleaming on their bayonets, the Virginians poured over the crest in screaming waves. The famed Rebel Yell was born at this moment, as hundreds of Confederate warriors out to kill or be killed erupted in a unique, bone-chilling war shout. They stormed into the disorganized

Federal ranks, and for the next hour, the bloody, hand-to-hand fighting surged back and forth until Jackson's brigade pierced the center of the Union line.

Hundreds of Confederate reinforcements were arriving on the left flank, some running straight from the train to join the charge against the Union line. The tired, hungry, and thirsty Federal soldiers could no longer advance or hold the land they had taken. Having lost 22 artillery pieces, which the Confederates quickly turned against them, they crumbled and panicked. McDowell ordered a retreat at about five o'clock, but an orderly withdrawal proved impossible and confusion led to a disastrous rout. Much of the army broke down into frightened mobs.

The Union troops splashed across the brown waters of Bull Run, climbed the steep banks, and jammed back across the Stone Bridge until a Rebel artillery shell exploded on it, in the center of a mass of soldiers. Southern cavalrymen lost their mobility in pursuit because they took so many prisoners. Surging desperately up the turnpike under Rebel shellfire, the dispirited Federals were joined by the terrified civilians who had come out to watch the fight. The load was so heavy that the bridge over Cub Run collapsed, disrupting the traffic even more.

Things were not sorted out until that night, when a full moon rose over the disintegrated Union army making its way through the streets of Washington. A distance that had taken three days to cover on the way to the battle was covered in a few hours going back. Then it began to rain.

A total of around 60,000 men, Northern and Southern, had been in and around Bull Run. General McDowell had commanded a Union army larger than the one Winfield Scott took into Mexico, but only about a third saw combat. The casualty figures are imprecise, but in that single day of fighting, McDowell lost an estimated 1,575 men killed and wounded, and another 1,200 as prisoners. The South sustained almost 2,000 killed, wounded, and taken prisoner.

Although it had been held out of the battle for hours, the 1st Virginia Brigade under General Jackson eventually suffered more losses—119 dead and 442 wounded—than any other Confederate brigade.

Long after the battle, Jackson went to an aid station, where the ground was covered by wounded men, but he declined medical attention until a doctor finished working with some badly wounded soldiers. The chief surgeon wanted to cut off off the mangled middle finger of his left hand. Jackson decided to have it set and bound instead, a procedure that was almost as painful as amputation. He paid little attention to the injury. Little Sorrel had also been wounded, but both man and horse fully recovered.

Whether the Confederates could have chased the defeated Union soldiers all the way back to Washington would long be a subject of debate by military men and historians. Although the Federals were in complete disarray, capturing the heart of their government would have been a tall order. The Confederates had the fresh men and supplies on hand, but they were just as exhausted and disorganized as the soldiers they were chasing over roads that the rain was quickly turning into muddy bogs. Since Johnston had stripped his command in the Valley, no more reinforcements were immediately available. The decision to strike for Washington would have had to be made at that moment, and the Confederate leaders chose to stop. Jackson, however, wanted to go. His philosophy was to never let a beaten enemy army escape total destruction.

Confederate President Jefferson Davis, who had come up from Richmond, thought at first that his troops had lost the battle. As he rode through the casualty station, Jackson, whom he did not know, stood and waved his little campaign hat, leading led his men in a cheer for their leader. He then he called out: "We have whipped them! They ran like sheep! Give me 10,000 men and I will take Washington City tomorrow."[7]

The victory had been great, for it had kicked the enemy army off the soil of the Old Dominion and made Washington fear invasion. General Patterson, so badly duped by Johnston's withdrawal, left the Army and returned to private life. President Lincoln also lost confidence in General McDowell and replaced him in overall command with the dashing young hero, George McClellan.

The day after the fight, Jackson wrote to his wife, "Whilst great credit is due to other parts of our gallant army, God made my brigade more instrumental than any other in repulsing the main attack. This is for your information only; say nothing about it. Let others speak praise, not myself."[8]

The headlines would go to Johnston and Beauregard, but public adulation would come to Jackson eventually. For the present, he had won the affection and allegiance of his men, who would now follow him anywhere, and also the respect of his peers. After Bull Run, he became "Stonewall" Jackson, and his tough Virginians proudly became the Stonewall Brigade.

Historian Bruce Catton observed that the brigade members were really no better than the thousands of other soldiers engaged in battle that day, except that they had Jackson as a leader. The English author Daniel Defoe once opined that it is better to have a lion at the head of an army of sheep, than a sheep at the head of an army of lions. Having a lion at the head of an army of lions proved to be a powerful combination.

CHAPTER 10

Second Star

HERE WAS A MAN AROUND WHOM AN ARMY COULD BE BUILT. A number of Confederate leaders proved their steel at Bull Run, but it was Thomas Jackson who made victory possible. In April 1861, when the war started, he was an unknown VMI major; in October, only six months later, he was made a major general, given command of an entire division, and then placed in charge of the new Department of Northern Virginia. His assignment was prodigious—the defense of the entire Shenandoah Valley, 150 miles long.

Jackson established camp near Winchester, the important community that controlled major turnpikes and a railroad at the northern end of the valley. To strengthen the handful of militia units scattered throughout the Shenandoah, Jackson received an influx of regulars, including the return of his own 1st Brigade, which he had reluctantly given up upon his promotion.

Winter was coming, bitter months that were no time for serious campaigning between armies of men on foot and horseback. Armies normally hunkered down in camp against the common enemy, cold, and stockpiled their supplies, trained, and readied themselves for the fights of spring. That was not the style of Stonewall Jackson.

First, he attempted to disrupt Union coal and other supplies moving to Washington by ruining a dam along the Chesapeake and Ohio Canal. The efforts did not have the intended effect, but they did lock Union forces to the area, preventing them from being put to use elsewhere.

Then he came up with a plan to hit Romney, a Federal stronghold about 40 miles west of Winchester, and before the end of the year, he led 10,000 men out on an expedition that began in good weather. By the first nightfall, however, they were wrapped in snow and ice. To march with Jackson could mean a marathon of hardship, and he scolded the Brigadier General Richard Garnett, the capable new commander of the Stonewall Brigade, for giving his men a long break for rations after 30 hours on the move.

They took the town of Bath in sloppy fashion, allowing the Union occupants to escape, and moved on, placing one frozen foot before the other, an icy wind biting through their uniforms and blankets. Jackson was more concerned for the feet of his horses than of his freezing men, and by the time the column stopped, the exhausted and sick soldiers were cursing him beneath their breath. Their complaints turned to surprise when cavalry scouts reported that the 18,000 Federals defending Romney had fled the city at their unexpected approach, meaning there would be no fight. Jackson left 4,000 of his newly assigned troops to guard the captured city and led the Stonewall Brigade and the rest back across the mountains to the warmth of Winchester, where his wife, Anna, awaited him. He arrived on January 23.

<hr />

The soldiers left at Romney, who had not been trained by Jackson, were under the command of General William Loring, a veteran but reluctant leader who had lost an arm in the Mexican War. Spending the winter in Romney was a horrid experience. As the men fell sick, a spirit of mutiny grew and idleness bred contempt of the man who, they felt, had abandoned them in such a pitiable situation—Stonewall Jackson. Senior officers wrote letters of protest to members of Congress, and several colonels signed a critical letter to Loring, who agreed that the entire campaign had been badly conceived and managed and had destroyed the heart of his fine fighting force. Jackson received the message, marked his disapproval on it, and forwarded it to Richmond. Jackson had already been unhappy with Loring because he felt the man was a timid commander in combat.

The discontent drew an unexpected amount of attention, especially when Loring dispatched a colonel to show a copy of the protest letter to influential members of the Confederate government. The remarkable document went all the way up to Secretary of War Judah Benjamin, Vice President Alexander Stevens, and even President Jefferson Davis. Having heard only one side of the story, the officials concluded that Jackson had made a mistake, and then proceeded to make a bigger one themselves. Bypassing the Army chain of command, they sent Jackson an ultimatum to pull the dissident troops out of Romney.

On the final day of January 1862, Jackson received the direct order and responded immediately that he had complied with it, but also that he was resigning his commission as a major general. He wanted to resume teaching at VMI, he said, because "with such interference in my command I cannot expect to be of much service in the field."[1]

General Joe Johnston was stunned by the interference of the civilians, who had left him ignorant of a decision that was about to deprive him of a talented general whom he badly needed. "I don't know how the loss of this officer can be supplied," he wrote, complaining to Benjamin that such civilian meddling within his military command could lead to disaster. [2]

An internal battle without guns swirled between the Romney insurgents and their allies and those who saw Jackson, the hero of Bull Run, as too valuable a man to lose. A separate campaign was underway to persuade the proud and stubborn Jackson to change his mind, something he was not inclined to do. Word of the growing feud spread within the Army, a potentially virulent disease that could sap fighting morale and corrupt the chain of command if allowed to linger.

Jackson finally relented and withdrew his resignation. Still, he was not one to suffer such a professional and personal slight casually, and he brought court-martial charges against Loring. By then, everyone else wanted the dispute to vanish, and no court-martial would be convened. Loring was reassigned to Georgia and his command distributed to other units. Loring departed, but Jackson would vividly remember another name, the man who carried the troublesome letter of complaint to Richmond, brigade commander Colonel William Taliaferro. Jackson had known him for years from VMI, but the friendship was now over. The two men would antagonize each other for many months to come.

+‑‑‑‑‑+

The internal workings on the Union side were not much better than those in the disorganized Confederacy. Over Christmas, President Lincoln had to extricate himself from the possibility of a second war by freeing two Confederate diplomats that Union sailors had taken by force from a British steamer on the high seas.

The Union awoke from the winter stalemate first and struck in the Western Theater, where its superior navy was prowling the broad rivers and Ulysses S. Grant was proving successful on the ground. Nashville was captured, and in the months that followed, the gunboats and the infantry also took New Orleans, the South's major port and largest city, and added other trophies such as Baton Rouge and Natchez. The western flank was particularly vulnerable because of its exploitable waterways. It was different in the east, although things grew dire for the Confederacy wherever the Union army and navy could link. A number of coastal forts were picked like ripe plums. The string of losses was demoralizing for the South.

The Union's problem in the east was that the new overall commander, General McClellan, a man who enjoyed parades more than combat, brought things to a halt while he endured a bout of typhoid fever. He also ignored accurate intelligence on Confederate strength in Northern Virginia, which placed approximately 40,000 Confederate soldiers in the area outside of Washington. He estimated the number to be five times higher. Planning to dodge the Southern force he imagined to be so powerful, he persuaded Lincoln to send the Army of the Potomac, more than 100,000 men with all of their equipment and supplies, from the Chesapeake Bay down to the eastern Peninsula of Virginia. On the water, he estimated, the supply line would be secure.

The campaign seemed to have promise when it began in March, and General Joe Johnston, outnumbered four-to-one, pulled back to within six miles of Richmond as legions of Union troops landed around Yorktown.

But when McClellan assessed his enemy in this area, he was wrong again: while there were only 13,000 Rebel troops facing him, he estimated the number to be about 100,000, far too many to attack. He dug in, pitched his tents, and called for Washington to send more men. Joe Johnston could not believe his good fortune and said to Lee, "No one but McClellan could have hesitated to attack."[3] The fearful McClellan's reluctance allowed Confederate reinforcements to arrive in time to help Johnston defend Richmond.

Meanwhile, far away in the Shenandoah Valley, Stonewall Jackson was about to begin a summertime rampage that would seal his name in history books and throw his shadow over the Federal capitol.

+===+

To move against Jackson, the Yankees sent a large force that would have been formidable had it not been led by Major General Nathaniel Banks, a former Massachusetts governor and ten-term congressman with a glaring lack of military experience. The badly overmatched Banks moved his 35,000 men across the Potomac during the first week of March and occupied Harper's Ferry and the surrounding region. This put him astride the northeastern mouth of the Valley, a direct threat to Winchester, where Jackson stood with just 5,000 Confederate troops.

Faced with such a gathering force, Jackson started to pull back on March 11, planning a surprise for his pursuers. He gave his senior commanders orders to place his wagons and men on the road out of town, which would draw the Federals into the area and give them a sense of confidence. After nightfall, Jackson wanted to whirl about and hit the unsuspecting enemy in a rare night attack, maneuvering by the light of a full moon. But his officers misunderstood the vague directions, the wagons and men moved too far south to accomplish the necessary spin, and Jackson lost the chance to grasp what he considered an opportunity to strike a unprepared foe. Riding away from Winchester, he grumbled that from now on, he would keep his plans to himself instead of trusting subordinates. "That is the last council of war I will ever hold!" he said, giving the false impression that he had actually sought anyone's advice. [4] For the rest of his war, he would remain true to that pledge.

Over the next week, Jackson retreated deeper into the Valley. He paused 18 miles from Winchester, at Strasburg, then moved back another dozen miles to Woodstock, finally coming to rest at Mount Jackson, almost 25 miles from Strasburg.

Confident that he had Jackson on the run, General Banks chased him with a beefed-up division commanded by Brigadier General James Shields, a multilingual former U.S. senator and a personal friend of President Lincoln (despite having once challenged him to a duel). But Shields was too slow, and by the time he entered Strasburg unopposed, he had lost track of Jackson, who was settling into the mountain's defensive position. Shields's reports convinced Banks that Jackson had probably abandoned the Valley altogether to join in the defense of Richmond. He ordered Shields to pull all the way back to Winchester, while Banks himself prepared to return to Washington, satisfied with his apparently successful campaign.

When cavalry scouts and spies within the Valley reported on the movements, Jackson, considering the opportunity too good to pass up, lunged out of his defensive fortress and became the hunter. He headed back toward Strasburg, but when he learned that the Union regiments were already passing back through Winchester and were headed up toward Harper's Ferry, Jackson went after them, hard-marching his men into exhaustion to try to take a bite out of the retreating columns.

The advancing foot-sore and hungry Confederates were detected just outside the village of Kernstown, south of Winchester, and Shields was incredulous. Picking a fight with a superior force was so unheard of in nineteenth-century warfare that Shields rode back down the line of his brigades to see for himself what Jackson was doing. When he appeared on a ridge, he was blown from his horse by a Rebel artillery shell and badly wounded. Command passed to Colonel Nathan Kimball, a brigade commander, but Shields continued to work from his hospital bed. Federal reconnaissance parties found only some Confederate cavalry in the area, and Shields and Banks agreed that Jackson would not commence a fight unless he expected considerable reinforcements.

Jackson was making plans to attack on Monday morning but changed his mind when he thought the delay might give the Union commanders time to recover from their surprise and reinforce. He decided to move immediately, which meant that his soldiers had to reach down deep to find the strength for battle after a hard day of marching. If Napoleon's men could to it, then so could his!

Hoping to turn the Federal flank, he threw brigades out to the east, only to find that the Union soldiers had stopped, formed lines, and prepared themselves to give battle. The element of surprise had disappeared. An aide galloped onto a high point, saw a field covered with lines of blue infantry moving forward, and notified Jackson that they were badly outnumbered. Jackson told him to say nothing about it, and an unforgiving fight soon erupted between the Rebel and Yankee boys, who pounded each other for hours.

Jackson caused confusion by issuing many orders and injecting himself directly into the battle, sometimes bypassing unit commanders and even going so far at one point as barking at a drummer boy. Finally, the Stonewall Brigade, with absolutely no ammunition left, began to crack, and its commander, General Garnett, ordered them to fall back. It was the start of a full-scale retreat that Jackson simply could not comprehend. His best men, his own brigade, had broken in the face of the enemy! They had not stayed to fight with bayonets! Jackson was enraged.

His men had enough fight left to prevent the Federals from pursuing, as Shields and Banks, still convinced that only a madman would fight without reinforcements, settled into defensive positions. The Confederates did the same.

With the battle done, Jackson arrested Richard Garnett, relieved him from command of the Stonewall Brigade, and filed court-martial papers. The popular Garnett eventually would be reassigned; he died fighting at Gettysburg. The morose brigade, which no longer cheered when Jackson passed by, was given to the stern Brigadier General Charles Sidney Winder. He received a very cold reception from the troops, who believed Garnett had done the right thing. Nevertheless, the impression Jackson had made with the Loring incident was amplified by his strong action against Garnett, and every officer now knew for certain that no one was safe from the general's wrath if his orders were disobeyed.

<hr />

Kernstown was a tactical battlefield defeat for Jackson. He lost about a third of his command, with some 80 dead, about 455 wounded, and a few more than 260 missing, and he was forced to leave some wounded behind during the retreat. Among those captured was his wife's brother. Federal losses were also severe, with 103 dead and 465 wounded or missing, but their percentage was much lower because they had so many more men. The Union continued to hold Winchester.

"It was reported that they were retreating, but I guess they're retreating after us," a young Confederate soldier observed to his commanding general. Jackson, stern but ever polite, replied, "I think I may say I am satisfied, sir." [5] He always saw things differently, and usually, he was proven correct. Kernstown would soon become a major strategic victory.

CHAPTER 11

Shenandoah Ghost

JACKSON'S AUDACIOUS DECISION TO CHASE AND ATTACK GENERAL Shields shook the Federal government, which suddenly viewed the Shenandoah Valley as a broad path that a Confederate army could follow all the way to Washington. By forcing the fight at Kernstown against overwhelming odds, he had mystified his enemies. They overreacted and, in order to contain Jackson, discarded the timetable for capturing Richmond. The euphoria brought on by Union victories in the West evaporated, and the focus shifted to protecting Washington against this new menace.

General Nathaniel Banks, who had thought that General Shields had the Rebels under control, had been planning to march the rest of his 25,000 men further south. After Kernstown, he recalled them back to the Valley. A division at Harper's Ferry went on high alert, which pinned them down as effectively as cannon fire. They wouldn't be going anywhere.

Further, President Lincoln ordered General Irwin McDowell, the Union commander at Bull Run, to keep his 35,000 men operating around Manassas to further solidify the Washington defenses instead of heading down to help McClellan.

The Federal leaders were seeing ghosts. If Jackson had enough troops to attack a superior force and threaten Washington, was it not also reasonable to think he might shift some of his many divisions to regain lost territory in the West, where the famed explorer General John C. Frémont had just taken over the Mountain Department? The "German Division," made up primarily of foreigners and recent immigrants, was dispatched to reinforce Frémont and was utterly destroyed during the long march by horrendous weather and terrible mountain conditions.

They did not stop rearranging their forces until they boxed Jackson in with three large armies. Lincoln instructed Banks, "The most important thing at present is to throw Jackson well back and then to assume such a position as to enable you to prevent his return." [1]

By protecting Washington so strongly, they stopped tens of thousands of troops from going to aid McClellan, hobbling his grand scheme to take Richmond.

Seldom in history has a single small battle like Kernstown created such havoc among its victors. In the South, people did not care about the tactical setback, for they had begun to realize that Jackson had delivered a stunning blow to the enemy. The Union was dancing to the tune of tone-deaf Stonewall Jackson.

＋══◄＋

During the first week of April, Jackson established his division in an area known as Rude's Hill, a secure refuge that afforded him access to the Valley Turnpike, which ran along the western edge of the Massanutten Mountains and provided paths to the important gaps through the Shenandoah walls and into the neighboring Luray Valley. For a general who liked to move, Rude's Hill was a good choice.

The only realistic entry point for an approaching enemy was a single bridge over the North Fork of the Shenandoah. If forced to retreat, Jackson would be able to fall back through the passes and reach the safety of General Johnston's army around Richmond. Nearby were another 8,000 Confederate soldiers under Major General Richard Ewell, West Point Class of 1840. Another Virginian, he had gained military experience as a hard-riding dragoon in Mexico and out on the wild plains of the West, and he possessed some personal eccentricities that were just as strange as Jackson's. For him to label Jackson "crazy as a March hare" [2] was a case of the pot calling the kettle black. Ewell was often exasperated at Jackson for not revealing his full plans, but they were compatible where it counted most and proved to be fierce fighting partners.

Stonewall Jackson used the down time to reassemble his damaged force, figure out what to do next, and apologize to his scolding wife for instigating the fight at Kernstown on a Sunday. He pled with Anna that military necessity left him no choice, and told her that he hoped the Heavenly Father would understand and see that he never had to do so again. The prayer would not be answered, and in the future, his troops would joke that if they were fighting for Stonewall, it must be Sunday.

The division was badly scarred by the casualties and by the morale problems brought on by the punishment of General Garnett for falling back at Kernstown. Jackson expected the Stonewall Brigade to live up to its name and fight like furies every time. They had disappointed him at Kernstown, and he had disappointed them afterward.

Another piece of unpleasant business was the promotion to the rank of brigadier general of one of Jackson's sharpest critics: William Booth Taliaferro. Very intelligent and from a good Virginia family he had sided with the unfortunate General Loring in the Romney affair. The promotion meant that another general was stepping into the sights of the grudge-holding Jackson, and Stonewall quickly protested that the former state legislator was nothing but a political appointee undeserving of an important command. Taliaferro would prove Jackson very wrong, but the military successes would not be enough to salve their differences.

Jackson also used the recuperative period to assemble a more formal staff, mostly made up of men he knew and trusted, a number of them with strong religious convictions and ties. For his chief of staff, he chose not a seasoned combat veteran, but the Reverend Robert L. Dabney, an old friend who was a fire-breathing Presbyterian minister and a professor at the Union

Theological Seminary. Dabney admitted knowing nothing about the science of war and was ridiculed by soldiers when he rode about wearing a cutaway coat and a tall beaver hat and shading himself with an umbrella. They soon grew to love and respect him, both for his fiery sermons and his fearlessness in combat. Jackson prized him most of all because of his total loyalty and grew to rely on the preacher too much. His deputy was young Sandie Pendleton, son of the brave commander of the Rockbridge Artillery, and one of the most capable staff officers in the army.

Another handpicked staff member was Jedediah Hotchkiss, a schoolteacher with a talent for map-making. Since people of that time seldom wandered far from home, maps of large areas were scarce, and Jackson grasped the importance of the young man. He instructed Hotchkiss to draw up maps of the entire Shenandoah Valley, top to bottom, and pinpoint the best places for offense and defense. Jackson now would have something better than his own memories of the Valley's topography upon which to base his plans— maps would allow him to see over the horizon and around the hills.

<hr />

The lull came to an unexpected end on April 17, when Union cavalry pierced a Confederate screen and captured the North Fork bridge across the Shenandoah. That opened the gate to the Rude's Hill position, and the Valley Army was forced to retreat. Jackson plodded along silently on Little Sorrel, the horse finding its own way while its preoccupied rider remained lost in thought. Union generals believed he truly had to be running now, heading straight south toward the Confederate lines around Richmond. They were wrong again.

Jackson instead moved east and tucked into another secure position in the Elk Run Valley.

When Shields lost sight of Jackson, he misread the situation and reported to Washington, only 11 days after the singular success in capturing the bridge, that he had no doubt Jackson was retreating to Richmond. General Banks agreed, and by the end of April, thousands of Union troops were being pulled back from deep in the Valley, both to reinforce the iron defensive ring around Washington and to delegate more troops to McClellan.

Jackson decided to attack.

He had been in close communication with General Robert E. Lee, who was serving in the vague role of military advisor to President Jefferson Davis, with Joe Johnston in the overall field command of the Confederate Army. Lee and Jackson now agreed to dart *away* from Washington and strike in the West to throw Frémont's army off balance. Jackson wanted more men, and although Lee told him there were none to spare, he gave him permission to employ Dick Ewell's division.

Jackson put his Valley Army of 6,000 men on the road running west out of Elk Run before dawn on the final day of April 1962, but soon became bogged down in syrupy mud and steady, pounding rain. Ewell brought his troops into the Elk Run camp without any knowledge of the overall plan. Jackson was telling no one, not even his generals, anything more than they absolutely needed to know, and sometimes not even that much. In fact, he said that if his hat knew his plans, he would burn it.

It took two and a half days of days of cruel marching for Jackson's tired and grumbling troops to reach Port Republic, which was only 16 miles southwest of Elk Run. That slow pace would never do for Jackson, who needed quick movement before his enemies could find and repel him.

Staunton, a vital rail center served by the Virginia Central, lay straight ahead, but the mucky roads and trails were wearing out his troops. In a bold move that not one of them expected, he got them out of the mud by going east through the Brown's Gap, which penetrated the Blue Ridge Mountains, and then doubling back into the Shenandoah aboard trains that delivered them to their original destination, Staunton.

Surprisingly, Union intelligence correctly read the complicated movement and properly identified Jackson and Ewell in their new locations. That helped Union generals to divine what was about to unfold, but only to let still another opportunity slip through their fingers.

Jackson gave his tired troops a rest and took time to have his hair cut and finally exchange his blue VMI tunic for the gray uniform of a Confederate general. Staunton was locked down by cavalry, with no one allowed to enter or leave, and on Sunday, May 4, a most unexpected group of reinforcements arrived. Jackson had summoned the corps of cadets from the Virginia Military Institute at Lexington, and about 200 of the boy soldiers marched briskly into the city to answer the call. If Richmond could not furnish reinforcements, then he would furnish his own. This created another controversy until he dismissed the cadets under the age of 18 who did not have their parents' permission. The rest were attached to the Stonewall Brigade.

A telegram from Lee advised him that General Banks was not pursuing Jackson at all but was instead retreating back down the Valley, probably to set the reinforcement dominos falling once and for all. Banks would send extra troops over to General McDowell, who could then proceed to send more to McClellan before the attack on Richmond.

With Banks easing the pressure, Jackson put his army on the move within two days and strengthened it by scooping up the 2,800-man Army of the Northwest, commanded by Confederate Brigadier General Edward "Allegheny" Johnson, a veteran of many wars. The news puzzled Washington once again. Was *this* General Johnson actually the General Johnston they thought was defending Richmond?

Now Jackson had about 10,000 troops on the Staunton-Parkersburg Turnpike, with Ewell lodged firmly at Elk Run to protect his rear. It was a classic use of the doctrine on how a smaller army should attack a bigger one by gathering enough forces to outnumber the superior foe at its weakest points. The idea had been around for centuries, but thinking about it and actually applying it were two different things.

+>=—=<+

Stonewall Jackson was going after Pathfinder Frémont, whose more than 15,000 men were spread throughout the rugged mountains and valleys of western Virginia. Jackson planned to bloody Frémont's nose, push him back, and make him waste time gathering his troops.

Union Brigadier General Robert Milroy commanded the advance unit of the Frémont army, some 4,000 men positioned only 25 miles west of Staunton. Jackson chose him as the weakest link. Milroy had already concluded that Jackson would not attack, because to do so, he thought, would leave the Confederate rear exposed; Frémont had not alerted him that Jackson had corrected that problem. To further confuse the situation, Jackson took his staff on a quick jaunt south of Staunton, riding in plain view down to Lexington and then circling back, telling no one where he was going and hoping spies would report the misinformation to the enemy.

On May 7, Allegheny Johnson slashed away Milroy's outlying pickets, and the Confederates gained speed as the weather turned sunny and warm. The following evening, they converged in the foothills beyond Bull Pasture Mountain, within sight of the crossroads town of McDowell, where General Milroy had his headquarters on the far bank of the snaking Bull Pasture River. A final source of confusion was that the tiny town of McDowell in western Virginia bore the same name as Irwin McDowell, the Union general on the far side of the state. Washington was having trouble figuring out ex-actly what was happening when Jackson suddenly reappeared like a recurring bad dream.

Stonewall Jackson spurred Little Sorrel forward with the advance units that took possession of Sitlington's Hill over McDowell, in no hurry to at-tack because more of his battalions were arriving by the hour. Holding both the tactical advantages of high ground and superior force, he sent scouts to look for even better positions to expedite an enveloping attack the next morning.

Milroy, a former Indiana lawyer, knew he would not have a chance if he waited until all of Jackson's men arrived. After planting artillery atop the mountain, he launched an attack of his own in the afternoon of May 8 be-fore the Confederates were set, falling primarily upon the 12th Georgia Reg-iment in the center of the yet-unformed Rebel line. His repeated charges and artillery barrages battered the Georgians and even drove the Confederates back in places. Rebel casualties were heavy—Allegheny Johnson himself went down with a mangled ankle—but it was a losing fight from the start for Milroy, as Confederate reinforcements kept marching over the hill to join the battle.

The wounded Johnson was replaced by General William Taliaferro, whom Jackson detested. That afternoon, Taliaferro bolstered the wavering line, relieved the bloodied Georgians, and drove off the swarming Yankees. By nightfall, the fight was over; Milroy burned his camp and retreated through mountain passes.

Some argue that the victory belonged to the lower-ranking generals such as Taliaferro, but this ignores the way Jackson made it all possible. He sent Richmond the good news with the succinct message: "God blessed our arms with victory at McDowell yesterday." [3]

Milroy's rear guard units set ambushes and put forests ablaze to provide a thick cover of smoke. Jackson admired the tactics his enemy used during the three-day pursuit, but he was not really searching for another battle. He was busy laying traps of his own for whenever Frémont consolidated his army and tried to drive back this way. He sent cavalry troops to block every road through the mountain passes by burning bridges, cutting down trees, and pushing down huge boulders. Frémont would spend two weeks pulling his scattered army together, only to discover when he wanted to move that his routes were blocked. The Pathfinder had to find another path.

Frémont was stalled all the way back at Franklin, some 50 miles from Staunton, and the important rail lines in Staunton were no longer under immediate threat. Stonewall Jackson turned his columns back into the Shenandoah Valley and once more disappeared from Yankee view.

CHAPTER 12

Foot Cavalry

WHEN JACKSON DISAPPEARED AT THE END OF APRIL, MOST UNION commanders believed he had finally forsaken the Valley. They could now get on with shifting part of the mighty army commanded by General McDowell south from Manassas to join McClellan on the Virginia Peninsula, and finally persuade "Little Mac" that he had enough soldiers to attack Richmond.

General Banks, however, felt a storm coming. He had been told to release General Shields and his 11,000 men, the division that had whipped the Stonewall Brigade at Kernstown, and once more, Shields went marching away.

The attack against Frémont at the other end of the Valley proved that Jackson was still roaming about, and nobody knew exactly where he was. Banks believed Stonewall would soon plunge toward his (Banks's) own command, which had been reduced to 8,000 men spread among the towns at the northeastern end of the Shenandoah, the very doorstep to Washington. Reasoning that the Rebels would come up the Valley Turnpike, he blocked that important road at Strasburg with the bulk of his command. The Union troops had ignominiously retreated back over uncontested ground before digging in while Confederate sympathizers hooted in derision.

+≡══≡+

Jackson had been temporarily stymied by the crude communications of the day. Telegraph lines hummed where available, semaphore flags waved, and couriers on horseback dashed about as Lee, Jackson, Joe Johnston, and Dick Ewell tried to communicate from their different headquarters, frequently misunderstanding one another. Ewell did not know to whom he was supposed to answer, but he was well aware of Jackson's reputation for crushing officers who displeased him. He wanted to attack the flank of Shields's departing division but decided to stay where he was, under Jackson's control.

Stonewall released the VMI cadets but incorporated the troops of the wounded Allegheny Johnson and came out of the western mountains to Harrisonburg, then headed up the Valley to New Market. Ewell left the Elk Run campsite and moved parallel to Jackson through the Luray Valley.

The fog of miscommunication cleared somewhat on Sunday, May 18, when Jackson and Ewell met face-to-face, attended church together, and then talked strategy at the little town of Mount Solon, despite Jackson's aversion both to working on the Sabbath and to taking others into his confidence. They decided to attack Banks. Contradictory orders from their seniors continued to pester them, but two days later, the Valley Army started to move, gaining momentum when Jackson suddenly turned east and left the turnpike to dash through one of the mountain gaps and join Ewell's columns in the Luray Valley. They headed northeast at a surprising speed, with the infantrymen sometimes eating up as many as 30 miles a day, in the process earning themselves the name "Stonewall's Foot Cavalry."

In the coming few days, Jackson would paint a tactical masterpiece. His 17,000 veteran soldiers and more than 40 artillery pieces were hidden by the long bulk of Massanutten Mountain as he maneuvered to drop a better than two-to-one advantage on the anxious General Banks, whose position around Strasburg had him pointing the wrong way, down the wrong road.

The town of Front Royal was located at the waterway junction of the two forks of the Shenandoah River, at the head of the Luray Valley. It was the southeastern point of a strategic triangle. Strasburg lay to the northwest, across the Shenandoah's northern fork. The upper point of the triangle was the prize of Winchester, to the northeast. Taking Winchester would again open the door to Harper's Ferry, the Potomac River, and Washington. It would have seemed foolish on March 12, when Stonewall Jackson evacuated Winchester, to believe that he would be back only two months later, stronger than ever.

The Rebels pounced on the 1,000 Union soldiers protecting Front Royal on May 22, cutting the communication lines so Banks could not be alerted. Confederate cavalry swarmed the area to sever rail lines and then feinted with a show of strength on the Valley Pike to hold Banks's attention. By nightfall, Front Royal was isolated.

The main battle there began about two o'clock the following afternoon, with fresh intelligence on the Union defensive positions delivered by Belle Boyd, an 18-year-old spy in a blue dress who escaped from Front Royal at full gallop to report to Jackson personally. Federal pickets were swept aside and Rebel soldiers captured the town itself, while the Union defenders made a brief but determined stand on nearby Richardson's Hill. Jackson attacked directly into the guns on the left flank and spun off cavalry to envelop the position from the rear and slice the communication links over to Manassas.

The Union commander at Front Royal, Colonel John Kenly, torched his camp and headed for the bridges across the Shenandoah, hoping to burn them behind him. The gambit failed when Confederate soldiers captured the South Fork Bridge without difficulty and managed to save the North Fork Bridge by throwing the flaming hay bales into the water. Hands and arms were burned, but the road to Winchester lay open.

The relentless cavalrymen chased the retreating Federals, catching Kenly's rear guard three miles away and routing them. Kenly swung his remaining infantry companies into fighting formation, but the Confederate horsemen, although outnumbered, charged without hesitation and broke the line. Jackson could not have asked for a more complete victory. At a price of 36 men killed and wounded, he had destroyed the Fort Royal defenders and captured the wounded Colonel Kenly, about 750 of his soldiers, and a huge horde of supplies. Best of all, Jackson positioned himself on General Banks's flank, making the Strasburg position totally untenable.

+➤═══◄+

More than a hundred biographers over the years have tried to capture the essence of Stonewall Jackson, but none has ever done better than Jackson himself did in a conversation with a friend. He said, "Always mystify, mislead, and surprise the enemy, if possible; and when you strike and overcome him, never let up in the pursuit so long as your men have strength to follow; for an army routed, if hotly pursued, becomes panic-stricken, and can then be destroyed by half their number.

"The other rule is, never fight against heavy odds, if by any possible manoevering [*sic*] you can hurl your own force on only a part, and that weakest part, of your enemy and crush it. Such tactics will win every time, and a small army may thus destroy a large one in detail, and repeated victory will make it invincible." [1]

He had found the vulnerable point and the enemy was on the run. Now he reached not just for victory, but annihilation.

+➤═══◄+

Some Union soldiers who escaped Front Royal reached Strasburg under cover of darkness and delivered the bad news to Banks, who began to abandon his positions before midnight. By daylight, the road out to Winchester was jammed with wagons and troops.

Jackson rushed units forward to hit not Strasburg itself but the Valley Turnpike nine miles south of Winchester. When they got there, they found Banks's wagon train slogging along.

The blue eyes of Stonewall Jackson again blazed with excitement. He left Ewell with a couple of brigades as reserves and struck out across rough territory without real roads, while the weather soured and mud began to suck at wagon wheels, artillery caissons, and sore feet. By the time he arrived at the Pike, the head of the Banks column had passed, but the road remained a river of blue uniforms. A Confederate infantry battalion began to shoot from behind the safety of a stone wall on the high ground alongside the road, and Rebel artillery opened up from only half a mile away, practically point-blank range. Wide gaps were blown in the panicked column, Rebel infantry outflanked escaping Union soldiers, and cavalry troopers stormed vulnerable points. The scene, Jackson would later write, became an appalling spectacle of carnage and destruction.

And he wanted more. Believing that this was the moment to strike even harder, Jackson pushed northeast toward Winchester, through the bloody path of destroyed men, dead horses, strewn equipment, and wrecked wagons. Ewell surged his brigades forward to within two miles of Winchester.

Perhaps there had been too much victory for one day. The weary troops were collapsing by the roadside, and some were tempted away by the treasures of abandoned supplies. Even most of the strong sabers of Turner Ashby's trusted cavalry turned up missing at a critical moment, when Jackson encountered the formidable rear guard left behind by Banks to delay the Rebels with ambushes and roadblocks. Still, he pressed forward throughout the night, ignoring protests of commanders who wanted to let their exhausted men get some rest.

Jackson knew that time was an enemy. He could not give the beaten and demoralized Union men a chance to regroup and fight from the vantage points in the hills around Winchester, nor allow the bigger Federal armies to come to the aid of the embattled Banks. By morning, he was spreading his troops west and southwest of Winchester, with Ewell moving in on the southeast.

Jackson rode Little Sorrel along the front lines, issuing stern orders amid the gunfire and pounding the enemy with brigades and regiments. Ewell did likewise on his right, and beneath the unrelenting pressure, the Union line finally broke. "Forward! After the enemy!" Jackson shouted, and his soldiers, finding still another reserve of strength, went charging after the fleeing Union troops. "Now, let's holler!" Jackson shouted. "Order forward the whole army to the Potomac!" [2] Soon the Rebel battle cries were matched by the whoops and cheers of the happy residents of Winchester watching the detested Union troops fleeing for their lives.

President Lincoln was tired of Stonewall Jackson. The man was supposed to have been hemmed in and defeated by superior Union forces, but instead he now stood just across the Potomac River, knocking on the door to Washington. Something had to be done, but going after Jackson would mean temporarily abandoning the strategic plan to send more men down to the dawdling General McClellan.

Perhaps, Lincoln thought, he could turn Jackson's startling victories against him. On the afternoon of May 24, while the thoroughly whipped Banks was still being pursued, the President snapped out orders to get almost everybody he had in the region on the move to trap Jackson and his army.

General Banks was to reform on the Potomac, while militias from several states were summoned to help defend Washington. Pathfinder Frémont would abandon his drive into Tennessee and move in from the northwest over the mountains toward Harrisonburg. General McDowell was ordered to wheel about and press in from the east. Frémont and McDowell would knife deep behind Jackson's line and join their forces, and then Banks would re-enter the Valley from the northeast. The Union troops would total about 60,000 men, more than enough to snare Stonewall Jackson and his pesky army of some 17,000.

A dramatic race was underway. Before they could trap Stonewall, they had to catch him.

Jackson gave his exhausted army the day off on Sunday, May 26, issuing instructions for chaplains to hold services at four o'clock. Exactly 48 hours earlier, Lincoln had dispatched the telegrams to start the encirclement.

While Jackson was considering how to deal with Harper's Ferry, where Union defenses were strong, the news arrived that Frémont was on the move, as was McDowell, and that Banks was already re-crossing the Potomac elsewhere. The Northern strategy was clear: Jackson had to pull out fast.

His soldiers, only partially recovered from the exertions of the previous week, now had to get back on the road. But they had learned to endure hardships and believed Old Jack knew what he was doing. The officers were usually as mystified as their men about the overall goal, but everyone would march when ordered, and this would prove to be the difference from Union troops during the days ahead.

Jackson's wagon train, groaning with captured supplies and stretching some eight miles long, led the way out on the rainy morning of May 30. The 21st Virginia troops came next, guarding 2,300 Yankee prisoners. Then came division after division of infantry, followed by the rear guard of cavalry. They marched all day and spent the night back at Winchester.

Scouts reported that Jackson's old nemesis, Union General Shields, was only a dozen miles from Strasburg, which was astride Stonewall's line of retreat. Shields, however, was reluctant to run into Jackson without having superior numbers, and so he held back to wait for another 10,000 men to catch up. Frémont was also converging on Strasburg but ended up being diverted from a direct march because all the passes and roads had been blocked by the Confederate raiders during the McDowell operation a month earlier. Nevertheless, Jackson was in true jeopardy, for he was still 40 miles away from Strasburg, while both wings of the enemy were much closer.

He had his army up before dawn, marching again. The last unit to leave the mouth of the Valley was the Stonewall Brigade, which stayed at Harper's Ferry until the morning to keep the Union troops in place, and then set out in a fast, forced march. In the next 14 hours, the brigade covered 30 miles.

That was where the discipline, the experience, the pride, and the belief in their commander worked for the Foot Cavalry. Neither Shields on their left nor Frémont on their right had the same drive and determination as Stonewall Jackson, and by pushing his men mercilessly, he made sure the Rebels reached Strasburg first. His last units struggled through town and escaped, with two major Federal bodies of troops only a few miles away. In the words of historian Bruce Catton, the mighty Union effort to entrap Stonewall Jackson ended in a "humiliating fizzle." [3]

That failure would be felt on the Virginia Peninsula, where George McClellan was ever so slowly edging forward and promising to attack Richmond soon. Then he made the critical error of dividing his army.

McClellan had moved two full corps of troops south of the Chicka-hominy River, which reached from the mouth of the Chesapeake Bay almost to the outskirts of Richmond. The rest of his army, and its commanding general, remained on the other side of the river, which was flooding and roaring. McClellan exuded optimism. As soon as the sun came out and baked the mucky Virginia roads hard, then bridges could be built, enabling him to cross the Chickahominy in force. Instead, violent spring storms brewed up and scoured away his plans.

When Confederate General Joe Johnston learned that Union General McDowell was still chasing Stonewall, he pounced on McClellan's split force in a swampy area, starting the fight that would become known as Seven Pines. Johnston's plan to sweep down on the Yankee flank failed be-cause bad weather, bad roads, and bad luck kept entire divisions from the field. Had he succeeded, McClellan's army might have been destroyed. In-stead, the two-day battle gained little for either side other than appalling casualties.

But it was enough to frighten McClellan out of his brief moment of ag-gressiveness. He still possessed the larger army but remained convinced that the Confederates were stronger than they really were.

The Confederacy also received a shock, for Joe Johnston was so badly wounded that he could no longer command the army. It was a historic mo-ment, for President Jefferson Davis handed the important job to his chief military adviser, Robert E. Lee.

Stonewall Jackson could not have been more pleased. He and Lee were a perfect match, both aggressive and both at their best in unorthodox offensive operations. In defense, they were shrewd, daring, and immovable. Thanks to the inconclusive Seven Pines battle, Lee and Jackson would come together, and the Civil War would be lengthened substantially.

⊹⊱━━⊰⊹

In the Valley, Jackson was heading down the macadamized turnpike toward Harrisonburg, burning bridges behind him. With the solid surface under their feet, the soldiers marched on June 1, and again on June 2, and again on June 3, increasing the distance between themselves and their pursuers. The Yankees were now extended uncomfortably away from their safe areas and growing concerned about their flanks as they penetrated strong Rebel territory in miserable weather.

Jackson, also encountering raging high waters and steady rain, veered southwest of Harrisonburg toward Port Republic, where a strong covered bridge arched the swollen North River. He was running out of maneuvering room, and although the bad weather was slowing his enemies, he knew it would not remain his ally forever. The bridge at Port Republic represented a pathway to a decisive outcome, be it victory or defeat.

His army, his staff, and Jackson himself were worn out. In a week, they had covered an extraordinary 140 miles in some of the worst conditions possible. The general sent much of the wagon train, the sick and wounded, and the prisoners on to Waynesboro and Staunton to get them out of the way. Hundreds of stragglers had given up and fallen out along the march, leaving Jackson with about 12,000 soldiers, all of whom were nearing the limits of their physical abilities when they learned that the long march was over. It was time to fight.

(above) *Young Thomas Jackson, without parents, grew up at Jackson's Mill in what is now West Virginia.*

(right) *Young U.S. Army Lt. Thomas Jackson during the Mexican War, photo taken in Mexico City in 1847.*

(right) *Major Jackson in 1851, when he left the army to join the Virginia Military Institute.*

(left) *Jackson was married to his first wife, Elinor Junkins, only fifteen 15 before she and their baby died during childbirth in 1854.*

(All photographs courtesy of the Virginia Military Institute Archives.)

The eccentric Professor Jackson in 1855, while teaching at the Virginia Military Institute.

Jackson married his second wife, Mary Anna Morrison, his beloved esposa, *in 1857.*

General Robert E. Lee, who believed in Jackson's fighting abilities even when others had doubts.

Flamboyant Cavalry General Jeb Stuart was one of the few who could make Jackson laugh.

The well-known "Winchester Photograph" of Jackson in November 1862, after he hastily sewed on a button missing in the right row, third from the bottom.

(below) *Little Sorrel, the general's famous horse, on the parade ground where he grazed at VMI after the war.*

Julia Jackson, the general's daughter, with an oval necklace containing a photograph of her father.

(right) *The final photograph of Lt. Gen. Stonewall Jackson, taken at his Chancellorsville headquarters a few weeks before he was shot.*

(below) *The Lexington, Virginia, gravesite of Stonewall Jackson in 1886.*

The Stonewall Jackson statue at VMI.

CHAPTER 13

The Bridge

DAWN RARELY FOUND STONEWALL JACKSON ASLEEP, ALTHOUGH HE desperately needed rest. There was too much to do and too little time. Frémont was coming along the Valley Pike with 15,000 men, while Shields was approaching through the Luray, on the east side of Massanuten Mountain. The two-pronged maneuver was a reversal of the same tactic Jackson and Ewell had used so effectively going the other way only a few weeks before. This time Jackson would direct the defense, and he knew how to do it.

As long as he could keep the two enemy forces apart, he could pick a battleground and whip them one at a time. Poring over the Hotchkiss maps to find an advantage, he was in no mood for mercy. When an officer expressed regret that three gallant Federal soldiers were killed in charging his regiment by themselves, Jackson snorted, "No, Colonel. Shoot them all. I do not wish them to be brave."[1] It was a cold-blooded, effective tactic, for the death of a brave champion terrorizes the weak.

Frémont moved closer to Harrisonburg on Friday, June 6, 1862, as Jackson headed southeast, clawing toward the Port Republic bridge.

Cavalryman Turner Ashby, who had been promoted to brigadier general in March and now commanded a full brigade, kept General Frémont moving cautiously to prevent him from overrunning Jackson's rear guard. Two miles below Harrisonburg, Ashby found a tall ridge that obscured the view of anyone approaching and swung into a blocking position. He placed the 6th Virginia Cavalry in front and let the other two regiments dismount, graze their horses, and rest while he prepared an ambush.

Nearby, Jackson watched General Ewell take up the main strong defensive position at the crossroads village of Cross Keys, less than four miles from Port Republic. Ewell spread three brigades along a forested ridgeline above the village. Five artillery batteries bristled near the small water barrier of Mill Creek and a washboard series of low, rolling ridges. Although they were mostly clear, the ridges were bordered by thick woodland that would both prevent Yankee scouts from seeing far ahead and channel the approaching attackers into the exposed areas.

Frémont would have to come down that road through Ashby and toward a collision with Ewell, which Jackson estimated would be more than enough to keep that arm of the pincer in check. Stonewall kept the rest of his army moving into Port Republic, a town that would become the center of his universe. He sent mapmaker Jed Hotchkiss up to the high ground to watch for Shields.

Like many frontier towns, Port Republic had grown up where waterways meet. It was the starting point for the south fork of the Shenandoah River, which flowed away to the northeast. Combining to create that big river were two smaller ones, and the broad North River was spanned by a big bridge that served the road from Harrisonburg and Cross Keys. Across the bridge, the road became Main Street, which ran through the rectangular village and on toward Staunton. The town faced the South River and was approachable by shallow fording points at each end.

On that sunny Friday, a break from the continuing storms, Stonewall Jackson and his staff clattered across the bridge down Main Street and set up headquarters at the eastern edge of town at the Madison Hall estate of Dr. George W. Kemper. The long train of supplies and ammunition rattled past and the wagon masters bedded down in the fields just outside of town, along the road to Staunton.

The fighting elements stayed on the far bank of the North River, north of the bridge, taking position along the ridges and bluffs that overlooked the village, rivers, and surrounding terrain. From there, Jackson could speed help to Ewell if needed against Pathfinder Frémont, or confront Shields coming out of the Blue Ridge Mountains.

Jackson knew that the key was the bridge, for should worse come to worse, he could bring his army across the river, burn the span, and leave the Yankees beyond the water barrier while he headed for Staunton or into Brown's Gap through the Blue Ridge. He had chosen a battlefield that served his purposes.

<hr/>

Colonel Sir Percy Wyndham came trotting through Harrisonburg at the head of about 800 Union cavalrymen around one o'clock on Friday afternoon. Wyndham was an arrogant, flamboyant soldier of fortune from England who had given himself the rank of knight on the basis of titles he earned while serving in the armies of foreign nations.

His scouts had not found Ashby's Rebel horsemen among the steep ridges south of the city, so the Englishman was surprised to see them lined across the road and into the thick woods on either side. Ashby yelled for his other regiments to mount up, and in minutes, hundreds of blue and gray cavalrymen broke into a simultaneous charge.

But Wyndham had been lured into an ambush planned by Ashby, and a large Confederate force hiding in a tall wheat field sprang up and blasted the unprotected flank of the charging Yankees, who were then slammed by Ashby's violent cavalry charge. The shocked Federals rolled back in confusion onto their reserves. Wyndham's horse was killed, and the colonel was taken prisoner and sent down to Jackson for personal questioning.

A short time later, Ashby blundered into an ambush himself. This time, it was his line that snapped and his horse that was killed. Ashby toppled to the ground but popped right back up and advanced up Chestnut Hill, waving his saber and calling for his men to continue the charge. Confederate reinforcements hit the Union line, which again broke, and the Federals this time fell all the way back to Harrisonburg.

The body of Brigadier General Turner Ashby was found among the 17 Rebels killed in the wild skirmish. The death stunned the stoic Jackson. Ashby had fallen to a stray Rebel musket shot, what is now called "friendly fire." Jackson had lost one of his champions, a loss that almost proved catastrophic.

+▷━◁+

Stonewall Jackson was showing strain from the long march in bad weather but no sign of serious illness. A man of delicate physical constitution in peacetime, Jackson behaved in wartime as if he were made of iron, continuing to punish himself with hard marches, long hours, extreme danger, and strenuous work. A cumulative weariness was taking a toll, and his taut nerves made him more snappish than usual. There is evidence that his thoughts were drifting, including a peculiar, rambling note he wrote to General Joseph Johnston about the events at Seven Pines.

> General: My present position is such that if Shields forms a junction with Fremont by moving west he will have to do so by marching within 2 miles of my advanced brigade, or else he must return to New Market. Should my command be required at Richmond I can be at Mechum's Depot, on the Central Railroad, the second day's march, and part of my command can reach there the first day, as the distance is 25 miles. At present I do not see that I can do much more than rest my command and devote its time to drilling. My advance brigade is about 7 miles this side of Harrisonburg. If Shields crosses the Blue Ridge shall my entire command, or any part of it, move correspondingly?
>
> While I rejoice at your success, yet I am grieved to hear that you are wounded.
>
> Very respectfully, yours,
T.J. Jackson
Major-General[2]

He also received a letter from President Davis denying him another 20,000 men as reinforcements, whom Jackson had proposed using to plunge directly through the Yankees and perhaps into Pennsylvania. Even while bouncing around in his saddle on the long hike back from Harper's Ferry, Jackson's mind had been whirring with plans that ranged far beyond the next few muddy steps and even the next battle.

The rejection from Davis and his anguish at the death of Turner Ashby added to the burdens of the tired commander, who was about to defend against a dual attack by a superior force. No matter what he wrote to Johnston, there was much, much more to do than simply drill his men.

The body of Turner Ashby, draped in a Confederate flag, was brought to Port Republic on Saturday morning, June 7, and placed in a private home where a brief funeral service was held. He and Jackson had often disagreed sharply over discipline, but Jackson openly praised Ashby for his endurance, daring, and heroic character and spent some time beside the coffin of the 33-year-old cavalryman before returning to the war.

Jackson spent the morning reviewing positions around Port Republic and then rode over to Cross Keys in the afternoon to check on Ewell, who had been given another 8,500 men but was still outnumbered. Frémont sent a brigade out to test the Confederate lines, and when it was driven back, the Union general decided to spend another night in Harrisonburg. Since there had been no sign of Shields emerging from the Luray, Jackson anticipated that Frémont would make the first major thrust the next day. He had implicit trust in Ewell and gave few instructions other than, "Let the enemy get very close before your infantry fire; they won't stand long." [3]

By the time the sun went down, Jackson had returned to Port Republic, which was quiet because nearly all of his army was on the other side of the bridge, over the North Fork. The wagons were spread out of town to the southwest, a long convoy of important stocks totally at rest and almost completely unguarded. A couple of companies watched the two fording points along the South Fork, and a handful of cavalry fanned to the east to scout for Shields. Few soldiers other than Jackson and his staff were actually inside the town. Those arrangements left the entire south flank virtually undefended as Jackson returned to Madison Hall for the night. Mental fatigue can be worse than physical fatigue, and an exhausted commander is prone to make mistakes, which is just what Jackson did.

Only six miles away along the South Fork, Union Colonel Samuel Spriggs Carroll was also bedding down. Intelligence had reached General Shields about Jackson's emplacements at Port Republic, and he ordered Carroll's advance detachment to rush forward and burn the important bridge. That would trap Jackson's army with the water at its back and no room to maneuver; the Rebels could then be smashed between the closing Union forces.

Carroll led 1,000 infantrymen, about 150 cavalry troopers, and a half-dozen artillery pieces on a sweep far to Jackson's right to the hamlet of Conrad's Store, where the evil weather immobilized them for several critical days. Jackson's men had destroyed the bridge at Conrad's Store, but Port Republic could be reached by following the river. When the sun came out and roads dried, Carroll moved forward and made camp on Saturday night just six miles from the target. Confederate scouts had not found him.

June 8 turned out to be another Sunday on which Stonewall Jackson had to fight. He had finally gotten some sleep and was up shortly after daybreak, expecting to attend religious services. Instead, he would have a close call with captivity. A Confederate cavalryman dashed up to report that Union cavalry troops had crossed the south ford and were moving his way. Jackson saw them coming, mounted Little Sorrel, spurred him into a hard gallop, and raced through a fusillade of musket fire to burst across the bridge to safety. Two staff members were captured.

Jackson thundered into the midst of a Confederate regiment rushing toward the gunfire, waving his campaign cap and calling for them to charge through the enemy elements. The general then rounded up more infantry units and sent them across also, chasing away the Yankee raiders and finally securing the bridge.

Colonel Carroll had been given a clear chance and he fumbled it. His scouts found the exposed wagon train on the outskirts of Port Royal and went after it instead, but some Rebel infantrymen and the Reverend Major Dabney, who was to have delivered the morning sermon, opened fire with some new artillery pieces, and the Federal threat collapsed.

Had Carroll destroyed the bridge when his troopers first stormed into town, they would have isolated Jackson's army and might have bagged General Stonewall Jackson himself, along with his entire staff and the invaluable train of wagons carrying ammunition and supplies. Carroll failed. Jackson held the bridge, which meant he could keep to his plan.

+≻══≺+

By the time the bridge episode was done, fighting was underway at Cross Keys. Frémont and his gilded staff members, fearing they were outnumbered, directed a rather timid battle, and despite isolated incidents of bold Federal leadership, General Ewell drove them from the field. Satisfied with that arm of the fight, Jackson turned his attention to General Shields.

The final battle in the Shenandoah began on Monday, a fierce brawl that see-sawed for long hours.

For reinforcements, Jackson pulled the bulk of Ewell's units out of the line before Frémont, leaving only about 800 noisy skirmishers behind as a diversion to keep the Union general convinced he was facing the same mass of Confederates that had bloodied him earlier.

All night long, the troops shifted positions, with artillery placed to rake the open fields Shields's men would have to cross. The wagon train moved out for Brown's Gap.

Jackson, running without rest, collapsed on a bed and fell asleep fully dressed, still wearing his sash and sword. When an officer entered the room a short time later, the general immediately arose and went back to work.

Rebel infantry units were still moving in when it was discovered that Jackson, despite his artillery background, had overlooked a small, high plateau that was perfect for big guns. Union pieces were emplaced on it, and the location became the focus for both sides as the battle commenced. Precious hours elapsed before those guns, which came close to turning the tide of battle, were captured in a frantic and costly bayonet charge. By then, Shields's infantry forces had massed and advanced to attack.

Then the advantage swung strongly to the Rebels as Ewell showed up with a steady procession of regiments from Cross Keys and slammed the Federal flank. The captured artillery pieces on the plateau were turned on their former owners to devastating effect, and the Union attack was broken.

Shields chose not to commit more reinforcements, while Frémont remained agreeably idle in Harrisonburg. The two Union armies did not join until Jackson allowed them to do so.

Having defeated both Frémont and Shields in separate battles, Jackson finally pulled back. He would have been vastly outnumbered had the two Northern generals managed to attack him as a single unified force. In that event, he would have been able to do nothing but run. But his aggressiveness in dealing with them one at a time and his correct choice of fields for the fights had led to a pair of significant defeats for the Union.

When the fighting was done and the last Confederate soldier had crossed the covered bridge into Port Republic, the span was burned, along with a ragged makeshift second bridge. Stonewall Jackson had been rash, brave, shortsighted, tactically brilliant, extraordinarily lucky, aggressive, and unreasonably certain of the outcome. And he had won again.

⊦⊨═◄⊦

President Abraham Lincoln understood the situation better than his generals. The failure to trap Jackson helped him realize that Union armies could chase the man all over the countryside without really settling anything, just wasting men, ammunition, stocks, and time. What he called "Jackson's game" was a major sideshow that was causing "constant alarms [to] keep three or four times as many of our troops away from Richmond as his own force amounts to."[4] Leaving only the armies of Generals Banks and McDowell to protect against the possibility of Jackson suddenly coming out of the Shenandoah to attack Washington, the President put the Union focus back on defeating the major Rebel army, capturing Richmond, and ending the war.

CHAPTER 14

Under a Spell

THROUGHOUT EARLY 1862, THE SOUTH SUSTAINED SEVERE SET-backs, from losing vital port cities, to suffering a disastrous loss at Shiloh, to having General McClellan snailing along toward Richmond. Against such a bleak backdrop, the stirring tales of Stonewall and his heroic fellows in the Valley lifted morale for Southern fighting men and civilians alike. The Valley Campaign was a masterful operation in which an army that never numbered more than 17,000 soldiers outmarched, outfoxed, outfought, and neutralized forces three times its size.

But the heroes were worn out after their spectacular campaign to protect the western approaches to Richmond. They had marched 400 miles in 40 days, and while they had inflicted some 7,000 Union casualties, they had also suffered 2,700 of their own, including 800 at Port Republic. After that final fight, Jackson moved his men through the Blue Ridge Mountains and into the quiet forests near Weyer's Cave, a natural geologic showplace known today as the Grand Caverns.

For the Valley Army, it was an Elysian place of peace and quiet, and on June 12, their general allowed them five days off. One officer wrote a family member, "It appears to me now that fighting is becoming quite fashionable, especially in Jackson's army. We have had three days rest in the last two months—the balance of the time either on a forced march or fighting."[1]

The long, arduous campaign had drained Jackson physically and mentally. Apparently it had not dawned upon him that he was in fact human and not really a stone wall. Combat drains energy at an enormous rate, and continuous combat demands that a commander find time for rest. Ancient pikeman or modern general, every man must sleep sooner or later.

Still, while his men got some rest, Jackson barely slowed down. Lee had sent him three fresh brigades, about 7,000 men, and there had been some consideration of turning Stonewall loose to attack into Pennsylvania and Maryland. Lee decided against this course, but Jackson still wanted to go.

When Jackson sent an influential emissary to press his case in the capital, Lee quietly asked the messenger, "Colonel, don't you think General Jackson had better come down here first and help me drive these troublesome people away from before Richmond?"[2] Jackson obediently asked for his next order.

＋═══＝＋

In Washington, the strategic decision had been made to pursue the war around Richmond and let Generals Frémont and McDowell keep an eye on the Shenandoah. Although Jackson was no longer even there, he still owned the Valley. Frémont remained convinced that Jackson was moving to attack him, and McDowell was kept from marching his thousands of soldiers down to help McClellan. The federal commanders had been tricked so many times by Stonewall that they thought he was peering at them from behind every copse of trees.

＋═══＝＋

From the moment Robert E. Lee assumed command of the Confederate Army, he wanted to move against George McClellan. To defend Richmond,

Lee put his soldiers to work digging massive entrenchments outside the city, working them so hard that they called him the King of Spades.

McClellan was also digging about a mile away, convinced that his five corps of soldiers, some 105,000 men, were vastly outnumbered. Instead of attacking head on, he planned to float huge siege guns upriver and use them to flatten a path all the way to the capital.

Between the armies ripped the flooding Chickahominy River, which rises northwest of Richmond and rolls southeast for about 20 miles. The river was rampaging as badly in June as it had been during the spring. Bridges washed away, and the lowlands and bordering swamps became impassable bogs.

But there was a huge difference in what the two generals were doing. McClellan was digging to occupy holes in the ground. Lee was digging just to plant enough troops to hold McClellan in place so the rest of the Rebel army could maneuver.

To prepare his campaign, Lee sent the incomparable General Jeb Stuart on an extended scouting mission. Today, a helicopter would insert a couple of specialists in long-range intelligence, who would stay hidden while they gathered information and then be retrieved by the chopper. Stuart was no invisible commando. With his long red beard and an outrageous outfit that included spurs of gold, a French saber, and a cape lined in scarlet, he galloped off singing an Irish ballad at the head of 1,200 horse soldiers.

He went around the right end of the Union line near Mechanicsville, about 20 miles northwest of Richmond, and learned that it was defended by a 30,000-man corps commanded by General Fitz-John Porter. The corps was separated from the main Union body by high water and therefore vulnerable. Then Stuart discovered a massive Yankee supply depot due east from Porter's position at a town ironically named White House. He rode completely around McClellan's army in three days and returned to Lee splattered with mud but loaded with information.

Lee decided to slam Porter to tear out the anchor of the Union's right flank and then capture the supply center at White House. McClellan would have to retreat, and Richmond would be out of danger. Lee instructed Stonewall Jackson to arrive as soon as possible.

No longer having an independent command, Jackson only had to obey orders. No daring battle tactics were necessary, no strategy required on his part. All he had to do was move his men from Weyer's Cave down to the lines near Richmond. The task turned out to be almost more than he could handle, and it opened the strangest part of the Stonewall legend.

Seldom delegating authority and almost always keeping his plans inside his head, the exhausted general would inevitably stumble. The habit of working in his own private mental world turned against him. The only person he took into his confidence about the gigantic move was his close friend Major Dabney, the 42-year-old Presbyterian minister with no military training. Wrecking the chain of command by bypassing all of his senior commanders, Jackson ordered the shocked major to get the entire army moving. General Ewell was simply told to go to Charlottesville. Another general was frustrated at orders to retrace the route his troops had just traveled on the way to join the Valley Army.

Jackson had to be in Lee's headquarters on Monday, June 23, for a strategy meeting, but he wasted valuable time getting there and brought even more unnecessary pressure on himself. He left by train for Charlottesville and then traveled back to Gordonsville, where his infantrymen were arriving by a steady shuttle of trains. The general held them there for a full day while a rumor that some Yankees were nearby was investigated. He dined quietly with friends on Saturday night, showing no sign of urgency, although he was still about 50 miles from Richmond.

Sunday morning, instead of immediately heading out, Jackson decided to observe the Sabbath. His army of about 18,500 was spread over about 15 miles as the men, horses, mules, and wagons struggled east. Nevertheless, he declared Sunday to be a day of worship, and everything came to a halt. Jackson attended religious services with the newly arrived Texas brigade of General John Hood.

In order not to violate the Sabbath, he waited until an hour after midnight before setting out for the important Richmond conference, and then did so by horse, not by train. Dawn found him still in the saddle, and he did not reach Richmond until three o'clock Monday afternoon. By not traveling at least part of the way during the weekend and refusing to go by train, Jackson was becoming demonstrably erratic in his judgments. In Richmond, his West Point friend Daniel Harvey Hill, who had become Jackson's brother-in-law and also was a general now, discovered the weary and dirty Stonewall leaning against a fence in front of the headquarters.

In this sad physical shape, Jackson joined the other War Council members for a dinner at which he consumed only a glass of milk. Lee then laid his plan before Jackson, D.H. Hill, General James Longstreet, and another old classmate from West Point, General Ambrose Powell Hill.

Lee had decided to split his army. The network of earthworks before Richmond would remain manned by 25,000 Rebel troops to keep McClellan in place. That would leave Fitz-John Porter dangling on the Union flank with 30,000 men. Lee would move against him with 65,000.

Jackson, supported by Stuart's cavalry, would attack Porter's right flank. Once Jackson launched the attack, A.P Hill would hit Mechanicsville, and Porter would be under threat from his flank and rear. When A.P. Hill wheeled south, Generals Longstreet and D.H. Hill would also strike, and Porter would be forced from his positions. On a map, it looked like just the sort of aggressive move Jackson typically advocated. But the plan to concentrate a superior force at the point of attack was complex, and timing would be everything.

Stonewall Jackson was not only tired but also new to this swampy territory and without any trusted Hotchkiss maps for topographical guidance. He was new to the layered command structure in the general ranks, and to sharing responsibility and planning. He also struggled in a subordinate role, even under a talented handler such as Lee. "Jackson's genius never shone when he was under the command of another. It seemed then to be shrouded or paralyzed," wrote D.H. Hill. "This was the keynote to his whole character. The hooded falcon cannot strike the quarry."[3]

But he remained eager to fight. A substantial portion of the plan depended upon him getting to the starting point on schedule, and he even suggested accelerating the timetable. His fellow generals, concerned about the weather, enemy action, and unknown factors, persuaded him to build in a cushion of extra time. He agreed to take another day to get into place and attack at three o'clock on the morning of Thursday, June 26.

As the sun was about to set on Monday, Jackson left Richmond. Having gotten no sleep the previous night because of the long horseback ride to reach the city, he was now pounding back along rain-swept roads as a storm hovered around him. He rode 40 miles to Beaver Dam Station, arriving after daybreak at his headquarters, where he fell asleep before a fire, a book in his lap and his muddy boots still on his feet.

It was sleep, but not rest. Jackson was consumed all day Tuesday by the task of getting his columns of troops and wagons snaking along roads that were turning into quagmires. He still provided no precise destinations, nor shared what lay ahead with his senior commanders so that they could mentally prepare. Jackson's army moved 20 miles that day, an astonishing feat under such conditions, but with 27 hours left, he still had another 25 miles to go.

+⊷⊷+

They marched again the following day, Wednesday, June 25, and it was already dark by the time the front elements reached Ashland, six miles from the designated starting point, with the attack scheduled to begin in just a few hours. Stonewall called a halt to give his men time to rest and eat hot rations.

He stayed up preparing all Wednesday night, too, but admitted to Lee that he was not in position, citing the bad weather, and ordered his troops to be back on the move at three o'clock in the morning, the hour he had previously chosen to start the attack. Biographer Byron Farwell added up the fatigue factor and concluded that Jackson had "probably not had eight hours' sleep in the previous eighty-eight."[4] Combined with the incredible exertions of the previous weeks, Jackson had to be almost to the point of collapse.

+⊷⊷+

General George McClellan did a most unexpected thing on the eve of Lee's big offensive. He launched an attack of his own, sending two divisions toward Oak Grove, near the Seven Pines battlefield. McClellan was also preparing a major advance but had second thoughts when this early engagement foundered and became an unexpectedly heated battle. Oak Grove was the first of a week of fights that would be known by the cumulative name of the Seven Days.

That action so far to the south did not perturb Lee and had no effect at all on the northern end of the line, where the sluggish Jackson was approaching. The master of the quick march was at a virtual standstill. At dawn on Thursday he was in ill humor, as his miscalculation of the time needed to cover the distance was unraveling the entire ambitious timetable.

His army was disorganized and strung out. Many soldiers were still eating breakfast at eight o'clock, when the morning summer sun started to roast the soaked Piedmont and steam began to rise from the swamplands. Muck and floodwaters restricted movement. Union troops had blocked every approach with fallen trees, destroyed bridges, and other obstacles. After watching his troops struggle through such terrain, Jackson reluctantly notified General Lee that he was not yet at the starting line.

✛══✛

Stuart would be roaming on Jackson's left flank. On the right was a brigade under the command of Brigadier General Lawrence O'Bryan Branch, who was to link with General A.P. Hill. When Jackson attacked, Branch would notify Hill to cross the Chickahominy and drive through Mechanicsville. Longstreet and D.H. Hill would cross behind him.

At nine o'clock in the morning, although Jackson was six hours behind schedule, he still held hope for success and sent a message to Branch to move out and to notify A.P. Hill. Branch took his brigade across the river at the town of Half Sink and swung toward Mechanicsville, but the message failed to reach Hill.

Noon passed, and then the early afternoon hours, and no one but Branch had heard anything from Jackson. At three o'clock, the impatient A.P. Hill decided to wait no longer. He had received no new orders from Lee but believed that if he remained idle, the entire plan would be in jeopardy. He stripped for action, removing his tunic to reveal a red flannel shirt that would enable his men to recognize him easily, and then hurled his 16,000 troops across the river to occupy Mechanicsville.

Porter retreated a mile to emplacements waiting along the sharp ridges of Beaver Dam Creek, a narrow waterway with steep sides covered in thick brush. Hoping to dislodge the Yankees, Hill's pursuing soldiers became bogged down in ferocious frontal assaults, exactly what Lee had wanted to avoid. A regiment attacking at Ellerson's Mill was mauled, and a supporting brigade sent in by D.H. Hill met the same fate.

Stonewall Jackson reached the area around five o'clock in the afternoon. From Hundley's Corner, only about three miles from the fighting, he could hear rattling musket volleys and the throaty detonations of cannons.

Historians would long after ask why Jackson, of all people, did not immediately strike onward toward those sounds and crush Porter's right flank but instead stopped and put his men into a bivouac. One would note that the aggressive general's inaction was "one of the more frustrating mysteries of the civil war."[5] A Rebel soldier said later that Stonewall seemed so unlike himself that he appeared under a spell.[6]

The explanation for his strange behavior may lie partly with the vague orders Jackson received from Lee. The commanding general had him use two roads to reach the front, which split Jackson's force on the march and made it necessary for him to reassemble it. By the time he reached the area, it was late in the afternoon and probably too late for him to form ranks and engage before dark. Just as Stonewall Jackson expected subordinates to obey his orders to the letter, he scrupulously followed the instructions of his superiors, and General Lee had said nothing about advancing to the sound of the guns.

Jackson also had not heard from Longstreet, A.P. Hill, or D.H. Hill, and the steady firing must have puzzled him, since he was the one who was supposed to launch the big attack. Therefore, goes one analysis, he was just awaiting further orders.

There was no doubt that Lee had overall command problems. Not only was Jackson far behind schedule, but Lee also had heard nothing from either Longstreet or D.H. Hill. When the impetuous A.P. Hill attacked on his own decision, Lee sent an order to stop, but it apparently was not received. Lee was shocked when the casualty lists came in. Fourteen hundred Rebels had been killed and wounded on the first day! Union losses were less than four hundred.

By any tactical measure, he had lost this battle. But lessons were being learned. Lee was finding out what was needed to manage a large army and learning the dangers of making a plan too complex or issuing orders that were too vague. He barely knew many of his senior officers; communications that day were non-existent; and the commanders were making do with bad maps on unfamiliar terrain. Such problems could be solved. Jackson apparently was not yet aware of the shortcomings accruing to exhaustion.

Meanwhile, McClellan had learned that Stonewall was nearby, sitting up to the north like a wolf ready to pounce. The day's events had not even included Jackson, so what might the morrow bring when those Valley veterans got into the fight? Anxious about what Jackson might have up his sleeve, little Mac ordered Fitz-John Porter to abandon the strong Beaver Creek Dam positions and pull back.

Dazed and tired, the telltale fire dimming in his blue eyes, Jackson went to sleep that night unaware of his value as a diversion. His reputation alone had spooked the enemy.

On Friday, June 27, the third morning of the Seven Days, Jackson was informed by A.P. Hill that the Federals were now dug in around Gaines's Mill on Powhite Creek. Then Lee found him for a private conversation at about 11 A.M., during which Lee sat on a cedar stump while Jackson remained standing, holding his battered kepi in his hands. Lee explained that the day's attack on Porter would have A.P. Hill in the center, with Longstreet coming alongside to hit the Federal left. Jackson was to take position on the other side of A.P. Hill, and General D.H. Hill would circle behind him to extend the Rebel line. They would all sweep together down toward Cold Harbor, turn the enemy's right flank, and threaten the supply route from White House. Again, it was a complicated plan, and the orders were vague.

Jackson spoke with some cavalrymen who knew the area and could act as guides. As always, he told them as little as possible, instructing them only to direct his army toward Cold Harbor, unaware that there were two towns with almost identical names—Old Cold Harbor and New Cold Harbor. Jackson was supposed to move on Old Cold Harbor, but he had not been specific enough with the guides, and they steered the brigades onto the road toward New Cold Harbor. It was not until Jackson again heard the thunder of artillery from an unexpected direction that he realized that he was far out of position, several miles southwest of his assigned point. Irreplaceable time was lost reversing the movement to find the correct place.

Critics would question both the sharpness of his mental state and his leadership style. Grogginess like his might not have been so noticeable in a lesser personage, but Jackson was commanding 14 of the 26 brigades in Lee's entire Army of Northern Virginia. His decisions and actions carried enormous importance.

━━━✦━━━

Long before dawn, General Porter pulled back another four miles to a new strong position near Gaines's Mill, his 25,000 men newly reinforced with another 10,000 Union troops. Multiple lines of infantry were entrenched on high ground, and artillery pieces covered the approaches. Rebel attackers would have to cross the flat marshy soup of Boatswain's Swamp while under a heavy fire that would grow worse when they tried to climb the sharp slopes, which were covered with prickly vines, tangled brush, and thick stands of trees.

The fight erupted about noon with Jackson's troops lumbering along the wrong road. An A.P. Hill brigade drove back Federal skirmishers, but that was the last easy ground to be gained that day. Skirmishing became hard fighting. Lee brought up General Longstreet on Hill's right, expecting Jackson to be there at any moment.

But Jackson was still going the wrong way, and without his presence, there was no reason for the Union defenders to extend their line to meet him. So wave after wave of Confederate soldiers broke on the anvil of Porter's defense.

When Jackson finally reached the area, he believed he was in compliance with Lee's orders. He put D.H. Hill, who had looped behind him, into a wooded area at the left tip of the Confederate line. To his thinking, the troops of A.P. Hill and Longstreet would drive the Union troops his way, and his waiting divisions would pounce. Eight months later, Jackson would write a rather lame excuse that he had not pressed toward the obvious fighting out of concern that his troops might be mistaken for Yankees and be fired upon by the fellow Rebels.

It quickly became a repeat of the previous day. The torn ranks of A.P. Hill bore the brunt of the new battle, as Stonewall remained out of the action, and out of communication with Lee. Two messages from Lee had little or no impact on him. When some individual commanders took the initiative and moved to support Hill, their men were also chewed up by the savage Union fire.

Jackson finally sent three brigades into the field. The effort never really got off the ground, however, because Jackson made the queer choice of having Major John Harmon, his excellent quartermaster, deliver the complicated tactical orders by word of mouth to the commanders. Once again bypassing the chain of command, he thrust a junior officer into a position for which he was totally unqualified. Predictably, Harmon was unable to explain the orders, thus causing more confusion and delay. Jackson's men were not in battle formation and stayed put instead of moving forward.

The ongoing thunder of the battle seemed to steady him somewhat, and Jackson eventually got the brigades going in a piecemeal manner. Almost looking lost, he rode about sucking on a lemon. It was in this condition that Lee discovered him and gave him a friendly handshake and the mildest of rebukes: "Ah, General, I am glad to see you! I had hoped to be with you before!" The words must have felt like a lash to Jackson, who mumbled a reply. Lee continued, as if nothing was awry: "That fire is very heavy. Do you think your men can stand it?"[7]

Aides would later say that Jackson merely mumbled a reply, but that his eyes again started to show some life at what could be perceived as the challenge from his commander.

After meeting Lee, Jackson's orders became crisp and fast, and he rode Little Sorrel back and forth to grasp the desperate strategic situation. Fighting engulfed the entire front, with the Confederate units mixing and fighting and dying together. Union commanders seemed already to have carried the day, but Lee ordered a final charge about seven o'clock, with only an hour of daylight left.

The two armies clashed in a slugging match in the swamp and woodlands and fields. Units dueled, broke apart, retreated, and charged amid layers of smoke, the thick smell of gunpowder, the crash of artillery, the ringing clash of steel, and the Rebel yell. At last, Lee's field commanders began to come into their own, as Longstreet, the two Hills, and Jackson took charge. Major Dabney recalled that Jackson's "cheek and brow were blazing with the crimson blood, and beneath the vizor [sic] of his old drab hat, his eye glared with a fire."[8]

"This affair must hang in suspense no longer!" he snapped as he ordered division commanders forward with his familiar call: "Sweep the field with the bayonet!"

The Federal defenders had spent almost the entire day fighting and were now spent. McClellan had another 60,000 troops within reach but refused to commit them, ignoring the advice of other generals. Porter clung tenaciously to the high ground along the edge of the creek, turning back wave after wave of attackers, until the Rebel shock troops, big Colonel John B. Hood and his brigade of tough Texans, penetrated the center of the Yankee main line. Porter retreated across the Chickahominy to join the rest of McClellan's huge, idle force.

Lee and his lieutenants had won a decisive victory, although it came at the expensive price of 8,750 men killed, wounded, or captured. Union losses were 6,837 men, but the unnerved McClellan lost a lot more than men. He would now have to abandon the supply haven at White House and fall all the way back to the James River to hide beneath the canopy of the Union fleet's offshore cannons. His grand plan to capture Richmond faded with the cordite dusk.

McClellan whined in a rambling letter to Secretary of War Edwin Stanton that the government could not hold him responsible. His army was too small; if Washington would send just another 10,000 men, Little Mac promised he would be able to whip Bobby Lee. The message lapsed into self-pity and anger, but it was plain that McClellan was admitting defeat—though the ferocious Seven Days battle was only half over.

CHAPTER 15

Do Something!

MCCLELLAN PULLED BACK FURTHER THROUGH THE MORASS SO quickly that Lee's battered army lost track of him. The supply base at White House had been put to torch, but there had been too much material there to destroy quickly, and an immense quantity of Federal stores fell into Confederate hands.

There was no major fighting on Saturday, June 28, but the shadow of Stonewall Jackson fell over the faraway Shenandoah Valley again that day, as General Banks sent an urgent signal to Washington asking for reinforcements, feeling certain that Jackson was about to attack.

Jackson was not much of a threat anywhere at the moment, for he was at the edge of total collapse. He fell asleep while eating, while leaning against trees, and in the middle of conversations. Briefing officers could not tell even if he was awake when they were speaking to him. Without its leader, his vaunted army could do little, evidence of the danger of depending too much on one man instead of making sure others have been groomed to step into command if necessary.

✛══✛

Lee developed another complex attack for Sunday, but weather, bad roads, and unfamiliar terrain condemned it to failure before a shot was fired.

Jackson was to push straight across the bloated Chickahominy River. He inexplicably put still another critical job, repairing and building bridges, in the hands of someone unqualified, this time his trusted friend and chief of staff, the Reverend Major Dabney, who was not an engineer.

Lee issued instructions for his commanders to keep track of the Union forces, but the signal was so unclear that it provided Jackson another reason to stay where he was. So while Dabney struggled to construct river crossings, and Rebel and Yankee cannons barked at each other, Stonewall Jackson went to sleep for a few hours, awakening early Monday morning, drenched by heavy rain.

He got up looking like a wet and emaciated scarecrow in a filthy uniform, mounted Little Sorrel, and went to rendezvous with Lee. Rows of dead Confederate soldiers lay in nearby fields.

Lee greeted Jackson without rancor, and they dismounted and moved away to speak in private. Observers saw Jackson dig a pattern in the dirt with the toe of his boot, stomp on it, and declare, "We've got him!" [1] That bold statement was not followed by decisive action, however, and when Jackson's men waded into the White Oak Swamp and hit heavy Federal gunfire, he faltered. Nevertheless, he somehow found time to write his wife with instructions on how much money to give to their church.

Lee's new attack proved to be a bloody affair that concluded with the situation more or less unchanged. Scouts reported to Jackson on possible pathways through the swamp. Brigadier General Wade Hampton sat beside him on a pine log and advised him that a rude bridge had been completed and would take the Rebels to an exposed part of the Federal position. Jackson listened in silence, then rose and moved away.

Longstreet and D.H. Hill sent staff officers to plead with Stonewall Jackson to commit, but they found him asleep under a tree, his staff members unwilling to awaken him. That night, he fell asleep while chewing on his dinner. When he abruptly awoke, Jackson stood groggily and said, "Now, gentlemen, let us at once to bed, and rise with the dawn, and see if tomorrow we cannot do something!" [2]

The great reputation Stonewall Jackson had won in the Shenandoah was in tatters. Brilliant in the Valley, he was a failure on the Peninsula. Time and again, he did not show up where and when he was needed. Longstreet decided he was overrated, and A.P. Hill formed a grudge against him for neglecting to help. The one who counted most, however, was Robert E. Lee, and he did not lose faith in Jackson.

⊩═══⊣

As the Federals withdrew, their mass tightened like a fist. McClellan went aboard ship in the James River, and his men created extraordinarily strong defensive positions on Malvern Hill, a commanding height a mile long and half a mile wide. The big siege guns originally meant to bombard Richmond were hauled into place, and plateaus of artillery and infantry stacked up the slick, sharp sides to the flat top.

Against Malvern Hill, Lee began the final battles of the fierce Seven Days. Jackson led the advance down Willis Church Road and swung into a formation that put him on the left of the Southern line. On the right was his old friend and battery commander in Mexico, General John MacGruder, who had brought 15,000 men out of the Richmond defenses. Longstreet and A.P. Hill's weary forces were in reserve.

Its movements hampered by the terrain, most of the sparse Confederate artillery was blown away by Union batteries in short order. Waves of Rebel soldiers charged into the Federal artillerists and infantrymen. Here there were none of the grand movements, flanking gambits, or adroit tactics for which Lee and Jackson are famous, just men blindly charging up a steep hill. Historian Bruce Catton labeled it "one of the most tragic and hopeless attacks of the war."[3] To the bitter General D.H. Hill, the charge amounted to a mass murder of his men.

Throughout the fight, Jackson allowed himself to be sidetracked with details, dismounting, for example, to help pull a single artillery piece from the muck. Only when D.H. Hill pleaded for help did he send in more troops. By midnight, Jackson was asleep again, while out on the slopes of Malvern Hill, hundreds of young men lay wounded, dead, or dying.

Concerned about a possible counterattack, Ewell and D.H. Hill went to try to awaken Jackson at one o'clock in the morning. With the help of aides, they managed to get him to sit up. Somewhere in the core of his brain, Jackson was still able to think beyond the smoke of cannons, the moans of the dying, and the desperate pleas of his field commanders. McClellan "will clear out in the morning," he predicted, and went back to sleep.[4]

By daybreak, McClellan had done just that. There was still some more thrust and parry, but Lee declined to repeat the futile work of Malvern Hill against still another Federal strongpoint. The Union army recoiled beneath the safe canopy of the gunships, and the Confederates settled into new positions much further away from Richmond than where they had started. That was all the week of fighting managed to accomplish.

An accountant would conclude that the Union won the battle. The Rebels had 3,286 dead, 16,909 wounded, and 946 missing—a total of 20,141. Three-fourths of those losses came at Malvern Hill. The Union sustained 15,849 casualties in all—1,734 dead, 8,062 wounded, and 6,053 missing. But by the harsh measuring stick of war, Lee had won a huge campaign and saved Richmond.

━═━

The Yankees then made a serious blunder by letting Stonewall Jackson get some rest. More than a month elapsed before he had to face the Union army again.

Lee reshaped his Army of Northern Virginia by eliminating the command structure he had inherited from Joe Johnston. The war had grown too large in scale for a senior commander to direct brigade and divisional leaders, so Lee created two corps and gave them to James Longstreet and Stonewall Jackson. There was no better signal that he still believed in Jackson as a fighting machine.

Lee also turned to face northern Virginia, where the Union was amassing a huge force to march overland to Richmond. In mid-July, Jackson was ordered forward to counter the threat with 12,000 men. A rested Jackson, with independence of command once more, would more than repay Lee for his confidence.

⊬⊱══⊰⊩

Meanwhile, two heroes had been summoned from the West to save the Union: Generals Henry W. Halleck and John Pope.

Halleck overflowed with intellectual prowess. He was the holder of a Phi Beta Kappa key and the author of *Elements of Military Art and Science,* a standard text at West Point. He spent the Mexican War in California without entering combat, resigned as a captain, and became a wealthy attorney. The ancient Winfield Scott recalled him to active duty in 1861, giving him the rank of major general and hoping that Halleck would succeed him as the general-in-chief.

When that coveted job was instead given to young McClellan, Halleck moved to the Western front, where the aggressive success of subordinates masked his shortcomings: "Old Brains" was grand on theory, but he lacked battlefield brawn. When Lincoln abruptly fired McClellan in the middle of the summer of 1862, he gave Halleck the reins of the Northern armies.

Halleck would be the administrative head in Washington, while boastful Major General John Pope would be the hammer in the field. Pope had entered at West Point at 16 and won a brevet for bravery as a captain in Mexico. In this new war, he had defeated Rebel forts along the Mississippi River. However, he was so abrasive that he was heartily disliked not only by the enemy, but also by most of his own men, from privates to generals.

The old loose assemblage of the Valley's generals—Banks, McDowell, and the imperious Frémont—was newly christened the "Army of Virginia." The Pathfinder outranked Pope and quit in pique rather than serve beneath him. Hans Sigel of the German-American division replaced him. Pope had some 56,000 men, but they were spread over a lot of landscape, an invitation for Jackson to strike in the hopes of dividing and conquering.

The bulk of Pope's army was concentrated along the upper reaches of the Rappahannock River, which slices through most of northeastern Virginia for 184 miles before emptying into the Chesapeake Bay.

George McClellan, still idle on the Peninsula, was ordered to start shipping troops up the Rappahannock to support Pope. He dawdled, in part because Pope was a rival, but also because Washington had refused to reinforce him in his time of need.

Pope bragged about seeing only the backs of his enemies and told his troops to take whatever they needed from the countryside, an order tantamount to authorizing looting. This was followed by a string of other draconian measures, including requiring non-combatant Southerners living within his lines to swear an oath of allegiance to the United States, shooting them if they broke their pledge. When the directives filtered back to Jackson's camp, an observer commented, "This new general claims your attention." Stonewall answered, "And, please God, he shall have it." [5]

McClellan, meanwhile, mused that Pope soon would "be in full retreat or badly whipped."[6]

⊢═══⊣

Jackson arrived in Gordonsville, an important transportation junction where the Virginia Central Railroad met the Orange & Alexandria line and a pair of rocky roads. With no enemy pressure, the Confederate force spent several weeks during that hot summer resting unmolested around the hospitable community 65 miles northwest of Richmond. Jackson could step from his tent and see the crests of the Blue Ridge. General A.P. Hill, brilliant in combat but as difficult an officer as any in the army, had an ongoing feud with General Longstreet, once even challenging him to a duel. Lee defused the matter by transferring Hill and his "light division" of 6,000 men, actually the largest division in the army, over to Jackson. An eventual rupture between two such stubborn men was inevitable, but they would initially be a ferocious fighting tandem. Jackson's other divisional commanders were Valley veterans Dick Ewell and the stern and unpopular Samuel Winder. The overworked and ill Major Dabney hung up his sword, returned home to western Virginia, and never came back.

Jackson had some 18,000 confident, experienced soldiers, leather-tough survivors who had been tried by fire and were eager to fight. With the Valley army out of the steamy swamps, he regained the intelligence eyes he had lacked in the region. Information flowed in from civilians who hated Pope, and mapmaker Hotchkiss stayed busy plotting the area. Jackson's confidence soared.

Among the loose pieces of business Jackson used the down time to clean up was the long-delayed court-martial of Brigadier General Richard Garnett, whom he accused of dereliction of duty for letting the Stonewall Brigade retreat at Kernstown. He also intended to court-martial a colonel for pulling out of Fort Royal during the Shenandoah Campaign, but the officer resigned before a trial could begin. But this sort of tedious business immediately receded in importance when Pope began to move.

⊬═══⊣

Pope planned to sweep across the Rappahannock and down to the next big river, the Rapidan, in order to threaten the Rebel rail lines and the town of Charlottesville. He anchored the center of his army around Culpeper, and spread flanking divisions off to Fredericksburg to the east and faraway Sperryville to the west. When the Culpeper force advanced, Jackson spotted its weakness: It was too far forward, exposed and out of reach for a quick rescue from either wing. If he could crush the middle, the entire Union army would be separated, and he would be able to deal with the wings later. He was pleased to learn that the center was commanded by his old foe Nathaniel Banks. "He is always ready to fight, and he generally gets whipped," Jackson joked to his doctor. [7]

Stonewall put his divisions on the move August 7 with a daylong march beneath a brutal sun to Orange Court House, the county seat of Orange County. Geographically, they were almost halfway between the capitals of the warring nations.

Heeding Lee's advice to take his division commanders into his confidence, Jackson wrote orders for the divisions to move the next day along a single road toward Culpeper, 20 miles away. The orders were very clear: Ewell would take the lead, A.P. Hill's light division would follow, and Winder, who had been too sick even to get on his horse, would bring up the rear. During the night, however, Jackson changed his mind, and the rare clarity turned into chaos. A messenger was sent to Ewell with new verbal orders, but no messenger ever reached Hill or Winder. The resulting traffic jam of thousands of men, horses, and wagons took the entire scorching day to sort out.

Saturday morning found everyone back in order, covered with the white dust they kicked up as they marched. About noon, Jackson's lead elements forded the Rapidan and approached Culpeper. Brigadier General Jubal Early reported Union soldiers massed on a ridge straight ahead. Jackson moved fast, possibly too fast, and started the fight before all of his troops were on hand. Ewell's division was sent out to the right, while Winder's division, which had become second in line, headed to the left. Hill's powerful force, at the tail of the long column, had not yet arrived.

The predominant geographical feature in the area was Cedar Mountain, which was to the right of the road and bordered by a creek at the bottom. A farm sprawled across the flat land, fading away into thick fields of mature wheat and corn and on to heavy woods on the northwest side of the road.

Jackson sent the Jubal Early brigade forward at three o'clock, and although it was stopped by Union fire, the Federal pickets were driven off Cedar Mountain with surprising ease. Ewell secured the high ground to give Jackson a stable artillery platform and a firm anchor on his right.

The guns on the mountain opened up on the Union artillery emplaced on a distant ridge, and a two-hour duel erupted between the Confederacy, which had more guns, and the Union, which had bigger ones. One of the Federal shots killed General Winder, the commander of the Stonewall Division, and Brigadier General William Taliaferro took over just as he had done when Allegheny Johnson fell at McDowell. Jackson still thoroughly disliked him.

General Banks struck the center of the Rebel line with two infantry brigades that had been hidden in the farm's tall corn. Jackson spurred Little Sorrel to the hottest spot of the action, ignoring the thick musket and cannon fire. At one point, he told his staff to retreat while he stayed alone on a crest, watching the fight with a leg thrown comfortably across his saddle. He said the Yankees would not waste a shot at a single horseman, and absently brushed away the wood chips that showered him when a cannonball struck a nearby tree.

His busy mind was eagerly taking in the situation, and his visible presence on the front line gave his soldiers confidence. Few generals have ever led from the front like Stonewall Jackson, whose firm religious beliefs allowed him to be totally unconcerned about his safety. He trusted completely in Providence, convinced that he would die only when God wanted him to die, so he never bothered to worry about getting shot.

He brought a Georgia brigade into position, and the men cheered him mightily before charging into a battle that left them decimated but also stopped the Yankee threat to the center.

Jackson had guessed that most of the Union strength was to the right of the road, where he had a good grip on the mountain, but at about six o'-clock, another brigade of Yankee infantry came running through the wheat field on the other side. They slammed into the section of Rebel line that had not yet firmed up, and several brigades broke.

With the entire left side of the line wavering as more Federal units advanced, Jackson galloped headlong to the fight, jumping Little Sorrel over a fence in his race to the action.

He watched the mob scene unfold, hurried away to deploy A.P. Hill, who was just arriving, and then returned to his embattled, retreating troops. Jackson could not tolerate the sight of his men running. He tried to pull out his sword, but it was stuck, so he took off the scabbard and waved it overhead, slapping the frightened men on their backs and shoulders, ordering them back to the battle and roaring, "Rally, brave men, and press forward! Your general will lead you! Jackson will lead you! Follow me!" [8]

Stonewall Jackson then grabbed a Confederate battle flag and waved it, and as the new units pressed forward, the fleeing ones turned and joined them. These reinforcements were enough to stop the Union attack, but it was Jackson's personal and fearless determination not to lose that had rallied the spirit of them all. The dramatic episode restored the luster he had lost on the Peninsula.

Before the sun set, the battle of Cedar Mountain was over, and Stonewall had another victory. It was not enough, though, for he wanted to crush the enemy. He pushed forward in the night to chase the Yankees in the bright moonlight, but the long hours of battle had taken their toll.

Jackson reined himself in. He had learned the lesson of the Peninsula. Not only were his troops tired, but he saw telltale signs that he, too, was exhausted. He would not let his body betray him again. Later that night, he lay down on a patch of grass, refused some offered food, declared that the only thing he wanted was rest, and went to sleep.

CHAPTER 16

Second Bull Run

JACKSON CHOSE NOT TO HOLD CEDAR MOUNTAIN. HE HAD PICKED a fight on his own terms, blocked Pope's advance, and disrupted the Union timetable. As Federal reinforcements gathered, he dodged back across the Rapidan. General Lee left a thin line to defend Richmond, moved north with Longstreet's divisions, and reunited the Army of Northern Virginia on August 14 at Gordonsville in a council of war.

Jackson told Lee that Pope was camped about 20 miles away and vulnerable. Thousands of Union soldiers had crossed the Rappahannock, but not the Rapidan, and were now sandwiched between the two rivers. Rebels were in front of them, leaving a single bridge over the Rappahannock as Pope's only possible path of retreat. Lee decided to attack. When the meeting was done, Jackson lay down outside in a patch of shade and went to sleep.

The following evening, Jackson marched his three divisions off toward the Union strongpoint, only to have to stop and wait for three more days while the rest of the army maneuvered into position. The delay allowed Pope to recognize his vulnerability and pull back over the bridge. Lee watched through field glasses from a nearby hill as his chance for a crushing victory slipped away.

That night, the disappointed Jackson took a small group of staff officers and cavalrymen on an all-night reconnaissance mission, riding quietly for miles beneath a bright moon.

+>==--=<+

A gigantic tactical game of chess was underway as the Confederates sought to cross the Rappahannock. Jackson's old division, under the command of Taliaferro, led the way north and west, following the Rappahannock while the Yankees matched them step for step on the other side of the water. Jackson remained so close to the front of his Rebel column that when an artillery duel broke at Cunningham's Ford, he rode Little Sorrel among the barking cannons, an unnecessary and foolhardy move for a corps commander, but he simply could not resist going to a hot fight. The probe continued upriver on August 22, with Dick Ewell's division in front.

A crossing ford with no Union troops on the opposite bank was discovered near Sulphur Springs, and Jackson quickly sent infantry brigades and artillery pieces across. The shift was well underway when a torrential storm rolled in, causing the Rappahannock to rise six raging feet and isolating the Rebel troops on the Yankee shore.

The furious Jackson took out his anger at the elements by chastising generals, ripping up a mildly rebuking note from Lee about the exposed position of the wagon train, and arresting regimental commanders whose men had torn down a pretty fence for firewood. The high waters, a perceived breakdown in discipline, and his utter inability to make something happen soured him on everything. He sat astride Little Sorrel in the rushing river and stared morosely at the water sweeping past. It took almost two days before his isolated troops could be retrieved over a makeshift bridge and resume the movement upriver.

Jeb Stuart made another spectacular cavalry raid behind Union lines, barely evading capture but plundering General Pope's headquarters. The gleeful Stuart made off with more than a quarter of a million dollars worth of Federal money and confidential correspondence between Pope and Washington. He also stole Pope's hat and coat as trophies. Lee would soon read "the most intimate secrets of his [Pope's] numbers, his plans, and his pitiable embarrassments."[1]

Meanwhile, the Rebels slogged along the Rappahannock, with Pope matching their moves and waiting for reinforcements. Lee could not abide the stalemate, and made the bold decision to split his army again, despite being in close contact with a superior enemy force.

While Stuart and Longstreet staged noisy, bothersome probes and fake movements, Jackson stripped his divisions of all unnecessary gear and struck out under the cover of darkness on August 25. The march was ambitious, even for the Foot Cavalry, but Stonewall had long been itching to act.

His 23,000 soldiers were moving fast as the sun grew warm on their right shoulders after dawn and then fiercely hot as noon approached. The dust-caked Jackson rode among them, and they made 26 hard miles that first day, moving relentlessly through fields, paths, private yards, and creeks. Jackson was waiting beside the road as they entered Salem and the weary soldiers cheered. He ordered them to stop making so much noise, but confided to a staff officer, "Who would not conquer with troops as these?"[2]

Lee audaciously increased his bet and sent Jeb Stuart away from the phony front to reinforce Jackson. The horse soldiers rode all night.

+≻━≺+

Pope totally misjudged the situation: Stonewall Jackson must be heading back to the Shenandoah! Therefore, Lee must have enough men to feel safe dispatching Jackson. Thinking along these lines, he overestimated the size of the Confederate forces, as Union commanders in Virginia so often did. Pope had about 75,000 men on hand, and more coming, while Lee, who started with approximately 55,000, had just sent half of them marching away.

The stoic and silent Jackson kept his plans so close that even his divisional commanders did not know where they were going. When they disappeared behind the low Bull Run Mountains, he suddenly turned east and pushed fast through Thoroughfare Gap into the Union rear. By late afternoon, they had moved through Haymarket and Gainesville and stood astride the important Alexandria-Warrenton Turnpike. Stuart galloped in with his cavalry, and the Confederate threat behind Pope grew ominous.

Jackson aimed toward Manassas Junction at a fork in the road and sent Ewell down the left route to capture the rail town of Bristoe. A single train smashed through a hasty barricade, carrying the shocking news to Washington that Jackson was again at the door. Other trains were wrecked after the Confederates tore up the tracks.

Dog tired, the Rebels took the rich prize of Manassas and found that the junction town had been transformed into another huge Federal supply depot covering an entire square mile. Storehouses and railroad transport cars were stuffed with supplies of every sort: ammunition, artillery pieces, uniforms, blankets, and cigars. Horses, enemy soldiers, and runaway slaves were captured. The ragged Confederate soldiers gorged on a menu including everything from bacon and coffee to brandy and canned lobster. Jackson emptied casks of whiskey onto the dirt.

He had led his troops on an incredible 54-mile sweep around the right flank of the Union army without being detected, totally unhinging the methodical and arrogant John Pope.

+≡—≡+

The primary question for Jackson was how the enemy would respond, and by daybreak on August 27, four Federal regiments shuttled in by train from Washington came marching toward Manassas Junction, straight into the waiting Confederate artillery and a line of battle. Jackson was fired upon when he personally rode out to ask for the surrender, and the Rebels responded with a vengeance, opening up an attack that tore apart the Union ranks.

Pope took the bait, launching a counterstroke and forcing Ewell out of Bristoe. But by turning to hit Jackson, he lost track of the overall strategic situation. Lee and Longstreet were only 20 miles away and surging closer by the minute.

By the middle of the afternoon, a calm Stonewall Jackson left Manassas with two wagon trains bulging with supplies and his soldiers carrying everything they could fit into their pockets and belts. They set fire to the remaining supplies. Storehouses became infernos, as huge piles of ammunition erupted in roaring, earth-quaking explosions, and the dark sky lit up with the flames.

As with any Stonewall march, this one didn't follow a straight line. The divisions moved in different columns on different routes along Bull Run toward Centreville and into the woods, not only to mislead spies, but also because the secretive Jackson's terse, muddled orders were unreceived or misinterpreted. But about midnight, everyone was assembling again along a ridge near Groveton. Acres of pines and oaks offered cover for a fight and shade against the draining summer sun. Nearby ran the familiar Warrenton Turnpike. Only a mile from Henry House Hill, Jackson was overlooking the old Bull Run battlefield where he first became "Stonewall."

General Pope reacted to the reports of the apparently disorganized march by concluding that Jackson was retreating. He determined to give chase.

***

Robert E. Lee and the edgy, taciturn, and partially deaf James Longstreet were riding side by side, somewhat dismayed, at the head of about 30,000 men. Advance elements had already clashed with Federal cavalry screening Thoroughfare Gap, which surely meant that the advantage of surprise had been lost. Nevertheless, Pope made no move to stop them as they emerged from the Bull Run Mountains, and they sensed opportunity.

***

With the railroad junctions at Manassas and Bristoe destroyed, the turnpike appeared to be Pope's last line of retreat to a safe base. But Stonewall Jackson was in position right alongside him.

Under construction was a spur line of the Manassas Gap Railroad that would leave the main trunk line at Gainesville, cross Bull Run, and follow the busy Pike. It had not been completed, but a deep and long cut had been dug for the tracks, giving Jackson a readymade defensive position. While

Pope's people wandered about in the blistering heat, Jackson's troops rested in the shade and out of sight.

As an independent commander free to do what he wanted, Jackson orchestrated a superb combined-arms defense of infantry, artillery, and cavalry. His line was about two miles long, with A.P. Hill's division on the left, near Sudley Springs, Ewell in the center, and Taliaferro on the right with his flank anchored on Brawner's Farm. Behind them ran the high ground of Stony Ridge, where the Rebel artillery perched with measured ranges. Cavalry troops would roam the right flank and try to contact the Confederate main body.

Jackson lured Pope into a headlong chase, then turned and established strong defensive positions to rip the attackers. In the late afternoon, four Federal brigades, whose scouts had failed to spot the Confederate strongpoint, moved up the Pike. Jackson again trotted out alone to examine the marching columns and decided that a sudden attack on an exposed flank was worth the cost of revealing his position. With a mild order, he unleashed the Rebel troops, who came rushing from the woods as the artillery on Stony Ridge opened up over their heads. Incredible slaughter ensued, continuing until both sides were standing almost face to face, still blasting away.

Although the South held, the two-and-one-half hour battle was costly.

Each side suffered about 1,000 casualties, and Jackson lost two of his three divisional commanders, Taliaferro and General Ewell. Taliaferro sustained multiple serious wounds and Ewell was shot in the left knee and lost his leg. Both would recover and return to active service. On its surface, the battle seemed to be a tactical mistake, for Pope finally knew exactly where Jackson was. He prepared to hit the Confederates with everything he had.

⊢——·—⊣

Jackson knew better. He only had to hold until Lee and Longstreet arrived. During the night, on a long ride back toward Thoroughfare Gap, he put his ear to the ground to listen for the thump of thousands of approaching men and horses. He heard nothing.

He replaced the wounded Taliaferro with Brigadier General William E. Starke, who was young and still new to high command. Brigadier General Alexander R. Lawton assumed the place of Ewell, whose leg had to be amputated. The various fights of the past week had thinned Jackson's manpower substantially through death, wounds, desertion, and stragglers, and he now had only about 18,000 soldiers left.

To prepare for the coming onslaught, he drew his lines in tighter while maintaining the advantageous railroad cut and the bordering edge of the heavy woods.

The stumbling Pope was unable to sort it out. By dawn, the biggest gathering of Union forces was to the east, before the division of A.P. Hill, but the fight began on the far right end of Jackson's line, to the west, with an artillery duel. Jackson rode in, dismounted, and sat among the booming big guns to write dispatches while enemy cannonballs smashed the timber and plowed the ground.

Then came the chorus of Rebel yells that marked the arrival of reinforcements. And it was not just any unit that had come to the field, but the tough Texans of General John B. Hood, one of the best fighting brigades in the Confederate army, who joined on the right of Starke's line like another steel link in an already strong chain. With the arrival of Hood, Jackson knew his right flank was safe.

⊹══⊰

It was a different story on the left, where Hill and his men would spend the rest of the day fighting for their lives. They turned away repeated frontal assaults, but the charges damaged the line. Each time the Union troops fell back, the Rebels had to strip the dead of usable ammunition and even felt compelled to begin stockpiling rocks to throw.

A courier found Jackson on horseback, studying the Federal positions during a midday lull. General Hill sent his compliments to General Jackson and informed him that his (Hill's) defense was brittle.

"Tell them that if they are attacked again, he must beat them back!" Jackson snapped at the courier, then decided to see Hill himself.

"General, your men have done nobly," he said. "If you are attacked again you will beat the enemy back."

Even as they spoke, new volleys of musket fire and artillery marked the renewal of battle. "Here it comes," said Hill, and galloped away.

"I'll expect you to beat them!" Jackson called after him.[3]

The Hill line held again, and more Union dead were abandoned. But Pope still had plenty of men.

About three o'clock, more Yankee soldiers surged forward over their own dead, and the fighting turned personal. Killing was no longer done at a distance, but hand-to-hand, with rocks and fists and bayonets and useless muskets swung as clubs. Hill's troops wavered as Union soldiers gradually forced them back, and a Federal brigade under the command of one-armed General Phil Kearney broke through about five o'clock.

It had taken too long. Six brigades of Southern reinforcements arrived about the same time, and 2,500 screaming troops slammed into the Federal units to break the final Union charge of the day.

"I knew he could do it," Jackson commented with a smile when he learned of the critical event. It was one of the rare occasions in which he would give even oblique credit for a victory to anyone but God.

After six hours of ferocious fighting, not an inch of ground had changed hands.

<hr>

With the Federals pulling back to reorganize for the coming day, the Rebels also left their huge trench for the woodland behind them, where they would be concealed and safe. Jackson rode off to meet with General Lee, but Lee was not present at his headquarters, and Jackson fell asleep. When the commanding general returned, he decided not to awaken the battle-worn Jackson, allowing him to sleep the whole night through.

There was much to discuss, but it could wait until morning. The line was totally secure, and Longstreet actually had brought his divisions into place about noon but had resisted Lee's polite urging to join the fight that day.

The Army of Northern Virginia was rejoined, with Jackson on the strong left wing of a gigantic "V" defensive formation. Dozens of artillery pieces were in the center, like a hinge, and Longstreet's divisions were angled off to the right. One of the best ambushes in the history of warfare was ready to begin.

On the other side of the field, General Pope thought, incredibly, that he had won the battle. He learned that the Rebels had abandoned the railroad cut defensive positions and thought Jackson was using the night to retreat. He believed Longstreet was probably stationed in the rear to protect the Confederate pullback. Seldom has a general been so wrong, so often, about so much.

+≡≡+

As the sun rose, the Rebels remained hidden. Morning passed without action, then noon. Longstreet and Lee waited. Jackson sat on a fence while his men loafed in the shade. Pope smoked a cigar and leisurely gathered his units before starting the pursuit.

A single cannon shot at about three o'clock began the fight. When the Federal troops charged Jackson's apparently empty defensive positions, his men came back out from the trees and jumped back into the deep railroad cut, screeching their war cries. They decimated the first attack waves.

Robert E. Lee watched in amazement from among his still silent artillery batteries, as perhaps 10,000 Union soldiers moved against Jackson, leaving their left flank totally exposed in the process. John Pope had ordered a division to skirt the right edge of Jackson's line and cut off his "retreat." Instead, the Union horde was marching to certain doom.

At the other end of the line, Union soldiers were pressing hard against A.P. Hill once more. Judging that the time was right, Jackson asked for immediate help, and Lee and Longstreet decided almost simultaneously that there would never be a better moment.

Lee stepped out of the way, and the big guns opened up to blow jagged holes through the bunched together, unsuspecting Union troops. Longstreet's legions thundered in, and the trap snapped shut. The Union line collapsed in a chain reaction that rippled disastrously across the entire front. The pressure against Jackson vanished immediately, and his men, so overburdened during the past two days, came out of their positions to join the attack.

Lee's army pivoted on Hill's division at Sudley Springs and swept over the smoke-covered field, surging east along the Turnpike toward the Stone Bridge, slowed only by isolated pockets of determined resistance.

Once the magnitude of the disaster became obvious, Pope returned to his senses and orchestrated an urgent but orderly retreat. Two hours after the day's first fight began, he put together a makeshift defense that held Chinn Ridge for a while, and then made a final stand on the famous Henry House Hill at about six o'clock. Another thoroughly beaten Union army was soon staggering back over the infamous Stone Bridge.

CHAPTER 17

Harper's Ferry

GENERAL POPE RETREATED TO CENTREVILLE TO OCCUPY A SYSTEM of deep entrenchments the Confederates had built the previous year. Lee responded by sending Jackson and the foot cavalry out on another wide sweep to get behind the Union right flank. Pope had received 20,000 reinforcements, and Lee did not want to make a costly frontal assault, but he thought the flanking strategy might be enough to pry the Federals out of the strongpoint.

Jackson's battered veterans crossed Bull Run at Sudley Springs and headed north beneath wet skies that turned the Virginia roads into muck. They made only eight miles, but by the time they went into bivouac for the night, Jackson had control of the important Little River Turnpike, which led to Alexandria.

Jeb Stuart raided further behind Pope's extended right flank, causing some havoc and revealing to Pope that Stonewall Jackson was once again exactly where he was not wanted. The man was relentless! The Union general folded his cards and decided that the strong fortress of Centreville could not be held. He fell back to Alexandria, part of the heavy ring of fortifications around Washington.

There was nothing more for Jackson to gain. He did not have enough men to assault Washington, so with control of the Little River Turnpike and the enemy withdrawing, he could have rested his men and awaited the imminent arrival of Lee and Longstreet. Some other leader might have been tempted to loiter in the area, which was dominated by the war-ruined plantation mansion called Chantilly, but that was not Jackson's style. When the Union retreated, he would pursue. He would allow the enemy no pause.

The foot cavalry gathered the next morning beneath angry rain clouds, a hard wind blowing in from the coast. They moved down the turnpike until they reached the intersection with Ox Road, where Stuart reported Federals massed ahead of them.

Jackson planted his three divisions south of the pike, with Hill on the right and Lawton in the center, and put most of his artillery with the Starke division to the left. By the late afternoon, he was sitting hunched in his saddle, knees high to keep his boots beneath his rubber cape, about to spend the next two hours guiding one of his strangest battles.

He sent two brigades forward, and when they ran into the division of Union Brigadier Isaac Stevens, a fight erupted in the wind-whipped downpour, spreading as both sides fed in reinforcements. Thunder and lightning contested with cannon and musketry, and rain slammed down so hard that the opponents at times could not even see each other. One of Hill's brigades was separated from the main line, and Hill sought permission for it to retreat because wet gunpowder had made their weapons almost useless. Jackson sent word back for them to keep fighting right where they were because the Yankees' powder was just as wet. He expected every man who fought for him to stand like a stone wall on defense.

In the end, it was neither soggy gunpowder nor aggressiveness that turned the day and brought the furious fighting to an end; it was the loss of the commanders of two Union divisions. First General Isaac Stevens was blown off his white horse while carrying a battle flag. Then, in the glum, wet twilight, the talented Major General Philip Kearny mistakenly galloped into a patch of Confederate riflemen and was killed.

Those leadership losses, plus about 1,000 other casualties, threw the Federals into disarray. They pulled back beneath the cover of the storm, which was pounding with such ferocity that it took some time before the Rebels even realized they were gone. Jackson lost about 500 men, but had won again.

The overall casualty lists for both sides after the long Second Bull Run campaign were staggering, with the North losing almost twice as many men than the South. On the Federal side, 1,724 soldiers were killed, another 8,272 were wounded, and most of the 5,958 listed as missing had been taken prisoner. Casualties among the victorious Confederate army were almost as shocking: 1,481 dead, 7,627 wounded, and 89 missing.[1]

━━━━━━

In that bloody summer of 1862, the entire character of the war changed. Back in June, Stonewall Jackson, hounded through the Shenandoah by three Union armies directed by President Lincoln himself, was dangerously close to being annihilated. Southern cities were captured, the Union navy ruled the waters, and the Confederacy's commanding general, Joe Johnston, was badly wounded. A Union army was poised to capture Richmond.

But the knockout blow was not delivered, and against the odds the Rebels revived. They won the crucial battles in the Shenandoah, on the Peninsula, and, for the second time, at Bull Run, even as they regained lost ground in Tennessee and Kentucky. By the end of August, it was the Union that was staggering. Instead of being penned up to protect Richmond, Lee's Army of Northern Virginia was about to invade Maryland, and Jackson was again on the loose.

Jackson was the toast of Dixie. Moreover, ordinary people in the streets of the North and even of Europe recognized the name of the redoubtable and unlikely Southern hero and marveled at the fighting abilities of his rugged, quick-moving soldiers. This was no braided-up general resting on his gold stars amid pomp and military ritual far from a battle site. He was silent and humble, a deeply religious man who prayed each day and then went out and fought like the devil; an ordinary man who disdained personal glory, rode into the thick of the fighting on a rugged little brown horse, slept beneath trees in the rain, and wore a dirty uniform with a small-billed campaign cap crushed down over his head. Those common-man qualities, the impressive military campaigns, and the valiant nickname of "Stonewall" had thrust the general, at the age of 38, into international recognition. Many Union soldiers, even wounded ones, considered it a privilege to be captured by Stonewall Jackson. A Richmond newspaper frothed that he was "the most remarkable man in the history of war." [2] A London *Times* reporter shouted about the "universal wonder and admiration" for the general, comparing him to Oliver Cromwell. [3]

The likes of McClellan, Pope, McDowell, Banks, and Frémont had been shamed, and for the North to regain its footing, a change of command was urgently needed in the field. The frustrated civilian leadership decided on a veteran, popular soldier who had been fighting brilliant bureaucratic battles behind the scenes to paint a reputation for himself as a savior.

George McClellan replaced John Pope. Like him or hate him, and there were plenty on both sides of that fence, he was really the only choice the North had. Little Mac, with a gold sash around his waist, rode out to meet the retreating army being led ignominiously back into Washington by the dirty, defeated John Pope. The moment they recognized him, the beaten and dispirited troops broke into cheers. General Pope was banished to Minnesota to fight Indians.

<hr/>

The Army of Northern Virginia waded across the Potomac River on September 5, with the Stonewall Brigade band tooting "Maryland, My Maryland."

Robert E. Lee, with 45,000 men, knew he was too outnumbered to win a war of attrition. He would not wait around for the Union to build an even bigger army. Maryland presented an attractive target.

Rival armies had stripped bare the cupboards of northern Virginia, but the lush Maryland farmland was almost untouched and could supply food for his troops. Clothes and shoes awaited the bedraggled Southern soldiers in the cities and towns. The population was expected to be sympathetic.

Lee gambled that winning a few victories on enemy soil would disturb the delicate Washington power structure and strengthen the anti-war forces. If Lee pushed through into Pennsylvania, even New York would be threatened. England and France might finally intervene on behalf of the Confederacy.

The plan was strategically sound, but bad omens indicated Marse Robert's luck was running out. Lee himself had to cross the Potomac in an ambulance wagon. His hands had tangled with his horse's reins when the beast spooked, and Lee broke a bone in one hand and badly sprained the other wrist.

The famous Little Sorrel, Stonewall Jackson's favorite mount, had gone missing a few days earlier for reasons unknown. A large, beautiful mare he was given as a replacement promptly fell on him. After this incident, the aching Jackson was also in an ambulance for a while.

With the shooting war quiet for a time, Jackson resumed fighting with his own officers, no matter what their value. Nobody was ever safe from his wrath. Within a few days, both the battle-tested A.P. Hill and the new divisional commander, General Starke, were under arrest and removed from their commands for reasons that had nothing to do with their steady performances in combat. Hill had to march along like a common private, eating dust at the rear of his old division.

In addition, many troopers drifted away, having joined only to defend their Southern homeland and wanting no part of invading another country.

Jackson was impressed by the charming town of Frederick, Maryland, and wrote home to Anna that he looked forward to someday seeing ladies and gentlemen back in Lexington sitting on similar porches and looking just as comfortable. That Sunday, he attended a German Reformed Church, sat in the rear, and went to sleep.

His soldiers were among the first to arrive in Frederick. Barefoot men got shoes. Men with torn shirts and the seats worn from their pants got new clothes. Food filled their bellies. Robert E. Lee issued a friendly proclamation to the citizens: "Our army has come among you, and is prepared to assist you with the power of its arms in regaining the rights of which you have been despoiled."

Everyone did not welcome him. As modern planners misread the mood of the population prior to the invasion of Iraq, Lee overestimated the amount of support he would find in Maryland. The state was so awash with pro-Union sentiment that John Greenleaf Whittier wrote a poem about the widow Barbara Fritchie leaning from her window and calling out to the passing Stonewall to shoot her rather than ruin the flag of the United States. The poem does not describe a factual incident, but it does capture a sentiment widely shared at the time.

For the Maryland adventure to work, Lee needed to secure his own line of supply and communications back to the Shenandoah Valley. Stonewall Jackson was just the man for the job.

The Rebels had already cut between Washington and the Federal garrisons at both Martinsburg and Harper's Ferry. Accepted military tactics would have been for both of those isolated outposts to be abandoned; however, the commander at Harper's Ferry was under firm and direct orders to defend his vital position, so he did not withdraw. The troops in nearby Martinsburg also stayed.

+⇒━⇐+

Lee divided his army into four parts and wrote specific assignments for each in General Order 101. He planned to re-open the door to the Valley, regroup, wheel about, and stand against the approaching Union force that he expected McClellan to lead out of Washington. But Lee, aware of McClellan's habitual slowness, knew he had time. He sent General Longstreet to Hagerstown to block the main Union body. The other three columns set out for Harper's Ferry.

There have been few cases in which a commander was so suited for the job assigned to him. Stonewall Jackson knew the place like the back of his hand. The tactical lock on that town had not been changed since he first went there for John Brown's execution, or when it was his first command at the beginning of the war. From the start, he set out to control Bolivar Heights to the north, Loudoun Heights to the south, and Maryland Heights to the east. With those in hand, artillery would bombard the town until it gave up.

+⇒━⇐+

Major General Lafayette McLaws of Georgia would move through Turner's Gap in South Mountain and attack the Maryland Heights. Loudon Heights was assigned to the division commanded by General James Walker, a fighter so tough that while a cadet at VMI, he had threatened the life of one of his professors—a pedantic tyrant named Major Thomas Jackson.

Jackson would take three divisions in the final column, capture the Union overlook on Bolivar and furnish the infantry attack force. When the parts were assembled, he would then assume command as the senior general present. It would be his largest command yet—six divisions, 23,000 men.

To deceive spies, Jackson spent much of September 9 making inquiries about places other than his target area, and at three o'clock the next morning he had the foot cavalry hustling out of Frederick on a 14-mile march that took them through Turner's Gap and down to Boonsboro, where he again narrowly avoided being captured.

Up before the sun the next day, he changed his mind about the planned route without informing anyone and swung to the northwest instead of marching directly to Martinsburg. Of course, none of his commanders or soldiers knew where they were heading, but when they re-crossed the Potomac, only knee-deep at Light's Ford, the band struck up "Carry Me Back to Old Virginny." They made 20 miles on September 11, and A.P. Hill requested to be reprieved from arrest in order to lead the division in the coming battle. Jackson agreed. Hill, unused to marching, had been hobbled by a big blister on his foot and ended up climbing into an ambulance.

+≻══≺+

The approaching Rebel storm was just too much for poor old General Julius White, the leader of the 2,500 Union soldiers in Martinsburg. He had no experience whatsoever as a soldier and he was expected to stop Stonewall Jackson? Why, only a month earlier, White had been a customs collector in Chicago! He withdrew from Martinsburg and fell back into the bigger, stronger garrison town of Harper's Ferry, where he submitted his command to Colonel Dixon Miles, who was of less rank but someone White thought would surely be better at this sort of thing.

Miles, at 58, was the oldest colonel in the entire Union army. Despite having been convicted of drunkenness during First Bull Run and surpassed by younger officers, he somehow still held an important post. There were

12,500 Union soldiers, about half of them raw recruits, packed into Harper's Ferry, and they were being led by two fools.

⊹━⋯━⊹

The battle-tested Confederate veterans took Martinsburg without a fight, and were amused to watch the bearded and bashful Jackson awkwardly deal with the adoring women who pressed about him there. ("Really, ladies, this is the first time I was ever surrounded by the enemy!") Then they got to the job of driving Federal troops from the heights around Harper's Ferry. The smoothness of the operation may have lulled Jackson into letting the schedule slip a day behind plan, but for the time being, things could not have been better.

Then Jackson received an urgent dispatch from Robert E. Lee to hurry up. Something terrible had happened.

CHAPTER 18

The Bloodiest Day

LEE'S METICULOUS GENERAL ORDER 191 WAS FOUND IN A FIELD OF clover by a Union private outside of Frederick, Maryland, wrapped around three cigars. The document was of such obvious importance that it zoomed up to the hands of General McClellan within an hour.

"Here is a paper with which, if I cannot whip Bobby Lee, I will be willing to go home," Little Mac crowed to one of his field commanders as he reviewed the detailed Confederate battle plan: dates, places, strengths, commanders, goals, and even the rendezvous point, the town of Boonsboro. Lee's forces were divided and could be destroyed one piece at a time. All that was required was swift action, the one thing beyond McClellan's grasp. "Tomorrow we will pitch into his center, and if you people will only do two good, hard days' marching, I will put Lee in a position he will find it hard to get out of."[1] The key word was "Tomorrow."

He had surged north out of Washington with some 88,000 men but lost track of the Southern army when it vanished to the northwest, behind the long bulk of South Mountain. After the astounding discovery of the battle plan on the morning of September 13, the Union commander knew exactly where his enemy was, and was going. It was a general's dream come true.

McClellan let most of that momentous Saturday slide by before deciding how to start the new campaign to destroy the Confederate army. Stonewall Jackson at Harper's Ferry emerged as the top item. He would maneuver against the master of maneuver.

Late Saturday afternoon, McClellan gave Major General William B. Franklin a target. His powerful VI Corps of 18,000 men was to hit the Confederates on the Maryland Heights, the eastern shoulder of Jackson's envelopment. The Rebel General McLaws, with an 8,000-man division, was still wrestling artillery into position there. Franklin could slide in behind him and sandwich the Confederates between VI Corps and the Union garrison that still held Harper's Ferry.

Franklin was ordered to move out—first thing the next morning!

⊹━━━⊹

It is generally believed that the missing orders were a copy that Jackson had written to A.P. Hill, although how the papers went astray and were wrapped around cigars in a clover field remains a mystery. A Southern sympathizer learned of the development and alerted Rebel forces. The news reached Lee with the same rushing speed that it had reached McClellan. Lee reacted swiftly to mend the damage. Worried about McLaws's vulnerability, he sent the Georgian urgent pleas to abandon his perilous position. McLaws declined to leave before the job was complete, and Stonewall Jackson continued the investment of the city.

Franklin set out at dawn on Sunday and made good progress until he ran into the Confederate rear guard at Crampton's Gap, one of the two major passes in South Mountain. The closer he got to his objective, the heavier the fighting became and the slower he went, infected just like McClellan with a peculiar spookiness at the possibility of being outnumbered. Although he held better than a two-to-one manpower advantage, he settled into defensive positions for another wasted night. That allowed McLaws time to consolidate his position and start throwing shells at Harper's Ferry.

Jackson's troops were swarming to the town like ants to a picnic, applying pressure at too many points for a defense to have any hope for success. General

Walker had taken Loudon Heights. A.P. Hill was in position to outflank Bolivar. Stonewall's blue eyes lit up with pleasure when he heard McLaws start firing from the Maryland Heights. As an artilleryman, he knew the placement of each of the 50 big guns assigned to the job. He confidently messaged Lee that the important Union garrison would fall the following day, Monday.

+⊱══⊰+

Throughout Sunday, there also had been heavy fighting at Turner's Gap, the second great penetration through South Mountain and the path between Frederick and Boonsboro. The brigades of General D.H. Hill, with reluctant support from General Longstreet, stalled attacks by the Federal I and IX Corps until night fell, then slipped away into the darkness.

The Union had bottled up both important routes through South Mountain, but the offensive sputtered to a halt because McClellan failed to stress the need for urgent action. Alan Pinkerton, the spymaster who had served him so badly on the Peninsula, again provided him with the faulty intelligence that Lee had 120,000 troops, about three times the true number. McClellan shied from the confrontation, afraid of ghosts.

+⊱══⊰+

By the end of the day, Lee realized that all was not lost. The mountain gaps were no longer important. With Harper's Ferry, he had a safe route to the Shenandoah. He decided to make a stand in Maryland, and ordered his generals to hasten to the little town of Sharpsburg, a German settlement between the Potomac and a minor waterway called Antietam Creek.

+⊱══⊰+

Jackson concluded his textbook demonstration of how to envelop an enemy position. When his trap closed on Harper's Ferry, no back door was left open for escape.

Early Monday morning, A.P. Hill took the Bolivar Heights. His infantry advanced toward the town as the Rebel artillerymen on the three hills slashed crossing cannonades upon the trapped Federals. The fighting and precision barrage lasted only 90 minutes. It was all over by eight o'clock.

The Union commander, Colonel Miles, put out a makeshift white surrender flag just before one of the final blasts of Rebel artillery sheared off his legs and left him mortally wounded. General Miles, the Chicago bureaucrat, reassumed command and rode out in a resplendent uniform and mounted on a prancing steed. He gave a salute and surrendered Harper's Ferry to the very dirty General Jackson, who was again riding grimy Little Sorrel. The horse had been recovered, but the reason it was missing in the first place was never settled. When Jackson later rode through the streets, captured Union troops broke through cordons of Confederate guards and rained cheers and huzzahs upon him.

By surrounding the town and forcing the surrender, Jackson had won a major victory without great loss of life, something very rare in the Civil War. The toll of 21 Union men killed and 73 wounded in the town could have been much, much higher.

After notifying Lee of the capitulation, Jackson wrote Anna: "It is my grateful privilege to write that our God has given us a brilliant victory at Harper's Ferry to-day. Probably nearly eleven thousand prisoners, a great number of small arms and over sixty pieces of artillery are, through God's blessing, in our possession. The action commenced yesterday, and ended this morning in the capitulation. Our Heavenly Father blesses us exceedingly."[2]

The exact numbers of prisoners and captured arms would increase when the official records were completed. Harper's Ferry was the largest surrender in the history of American warfare to that time.

+≻══≺+

Victory did not mean true rest, however, because Lee was still calling. Jackson decided to leave A.P. Hill behind to sort out the surrender. There was enough time for a few deep breaths and for the fighting scarecrows to feast upon the largess of another Federal arsenal and supply point—food for their bellies, clothes for their backs, ammunition for their guns. After days of hard marching through mountain gaps and across rivers to reach Harper's Ferry, they cooked rations and got ready to move out again. Jackson, who had not slept for two days, took them off on another midnight march.

It was as important as any they had made. Each step taken during those dark, early hours of Tuesday, September 16 narrowed McClellan's advantage at Antietam. Jackson had two divisions with him in the lead. They would be followed by Walker's troops from Loudon Heights, and then by McLaws, who had come down from Maryland Heights into the safety of Harper's Ferry. A.P. Hill would follow when the surrender was complete.

+⇒⇐+

Sharpsburg was a neat, rectangular community laid out on both sides of the Boonsboro Road, which ran west to east and crossed the meandering Antietam Creek, which folded away to the northeast. The waterway was the rough starting front line for the opposing armies.

The Rebel line was already established. General Longstreet's right was planted on the creek beneath the town. The left of his line terminated about a mile up the Hagerstown Turnpike at a tiny house of worship called the Dunkard Church, because its German Baptist congregation "dunked" new believers.

D.H. Hill spread his men in front of where Longstreet and Jackson would link. Stonewall Jackson extended the line further to the left, anchoring his right on the Dunkard Church, then stretching north along the turnpike. His own left would be guarded by Jeb Stuart's cavalry all the way to the Potomac. He plugged in his brigades as they arrived after the 17-mile march from Harper's Ferry.

Artillery batteries were put on the high ground of Nicodemus Hill to the north, where a smaller forested area known as the North Woods formed a natural barrier against advancing troops. Across the Pike, about half a mile from the church, was farmer David Miller's sprawling cornfield, where Rebel soldiers were hiding in the head-high corn. Artillery was in position behind the West Woods, which overlooked the natural attack route through the field.

Beyond that lay the East Woods, where Confederate troops and artillery were hidden on both sides of the road. Another strongpoint was established in the private home of a farmer, in the surrounding buildings, and along the adjacent fence.

Jackson had some 7,700 men in position by three o'clock in the afternoon. The missing part was the strong division of A.P. Hill, which was still back in Harper's Ferry cramming wagons full of supplies and issuing pardons to the thousands of prisoners. They had to pledge that, when released, they would not again pick up arms against the South. Dealing with victory took time.

━━━

There was no secret that a battle was looming at Sharpsburg. Both armies had been moving into position for two days, and there had already been skirmishes and booming long-range artillery duels. Men in blue and gray eyed each other across the undulating plain of grass as they shuffled into position beneath bright regimental standards. Lee had about 30,000 men along a front that stretched approximately four miles. Just to the east, McClellan had some 75,000. That night, soldiers on both sides whispered about what would come the next day, and kept their weapons close. Artillery barked and skirmishers bumped around in a light rain. Stonewall Jackson slept beneath a tree.

━━━

Union General Joseph "Fighting Joe" Hooker, a lean, trim man on a snow-white charger, had replaced the ineffective McDowell at the head of the Federal I Corps. He kicked off the battle by falling on the left edge of Jackson's line at six o'clock in the morning. The overnight rain had left behind a ground fog so thick that Jackson's men could not see the enemy, but only hear the splashing boots of Federal soldiers. A push down the pike by Federal skirmishers had been stopped the previous evening by concentrated Rebel fire from Nicodemus Hill, the woods, and the cornfield, so Hooker decided to put his big guns to work. Union cannons opened up with a roar on the cornfield, and artillery pieces from both sides sang in blazing chorus.

The bloodiest day of the Civil War was underway.

━━━

The frightful barrage pounded the defenseless Rebel soldiers in the cornfield, while Union infantrymen blazed away, the Yankee gunfire scything the corn down to dirt level.

When the barrage lifted and the smoke and fog cleared, Federal infantrymen stepped slowly out of the North Woods, an almost hypnotizing vision of long, precise lines of blue uniformed soldiers with morning sun-light shining on their bayonets. Now that the Confederate cornfield position had been pulverized, the next target was the farmhouse and fence strong-point. The defenders fought back with withering fire, but the Yankees first took the house, then broke the Rebels along the fence line, and finally forced them out of both the East and West Woods.

As the Federals pushed toward the Dunkard Church, they disturbed a hornets' nest of Texans. General John Hood's two brigades had been tem-porarily relieved from the line for a brief rest and some breakfast, including a meat ration, and they were furious when they had to abandon their meal to go fight the Yankee threat at seven o'clock. Hood was already mad because he had to be released by Lee after Longstreet put him under arrest over a minor dispute. The Texans opened with volleys of fire on the flank, then charged the unsteady Union troops with a fierce Rebel yell.

Not having to face the full enemy force along the entire line, Lee was able to answer Jackson's call for reinforcements, shifting in units from other parts of the line that were not under enemy pressure.

The Federal attack crumbled and fell back along the gruesome turnpike and through the grotesque cornfield. Before artillery blocked the Confeder-ates chasing the Union troops, things had almost returned to where they were at the start of the day. General Hooker lost almost half of his men and was himself so badly wounded in the foot that he had to leave his command. His I Corps, 8,800 strong, had been decimated and was now out of the fight.

In the East Wood and the West Wood, around the Dunkard Church and in Miller's field of corn, hundreds of blue-clad bodies lay in ranks where they had fallen among similarly sad groups of bloodied gray uniforms.

It was only the first battle of the day, and already some 5,000 men had fallen.

<hr/>

Jackson was being a stone wall again, and the line along the Pike remained in Rebel possession. He showed no hint of fear as he surveyed the raging battle.

The Reverend Dabney wrote in his biography that, "During this terrible conflict, General Jackson exposed his life with his accustomed imperturbable bravery, riding among his batteries and directing their fire, and communicating his own indomitable spirit to his men. Yet he said to a Christian comrade, that on no day of battle had he ever felt so calm an assurance that he should be preserved from all personal harm through the protection of his Heavenly Father." [3]

Not all leaders had such protection. Six brigadier and major generals, three from each side, were killed outright or mortally wounded at Antietam. Among them was General William Starke of the Stonewall Division. Another dozen, again half from blue and half from gray, were wounded. Regimental commanders fell like leaves. Starke was replaced by the Colonel Andrew Jackson Grigsby of the 27th Virginia, the Valley Brigade.

+≻═≺+

From his headquarters in a nice brick home on a hill two and a half miles from the church, McClellan decided to try Jackson again. He sent in the 8,000 men commanded by General Joseph Mansfield, who had replaced Jackson's favorite whipping boy, General Nathaniel Banks, as head of the XII Corps. Mansfield was mortally wounded before the fight really started.

The two Union divisions pushed the weakened Confederates back through the West Woods and the cornfield, but were stopped in desperate man-to-man fighting around the church. After a furious 90-minute battle, both sides broke contact, and there was a pause in the fighting along the Jackson front.

What was left of XII Corps joined the ruined I Corps on the Union wreckage heap. Both corps commanders—Major Generals Mansfield and Hooker—were dead or wounded. Stonewall Jackson was still standing.

+≻═≺+

Sensing that the Southern line was unsteady after the repeated attacks, McClellan threw what he believed would be the final punch, a beefy corps led by crusty 65-year-old General Edwin V. Sumner. McClellan did not brief him on what lay ahead on that tragic field.

Sumner moved toward the West Woods, not with his full complement of four divisions, but with 6,000 men who advanced in lines 500 yards long. Meeting little opposition, they did not actively patrol their flanks, walking straight into a curving spot in the Confederate line that exposed the Union flanks and rear. The unplanned Rebel crossfire ambush smashed the Yankee soldiers so hard that the woods appeared to be aflame. After 2,355 Federal soldiers were killed or wounded within a span of a few minutes, the remainder bolted, chased by screaming Rebels for about half a mile.

That marked the end of fierce combat along Jackson's immediate front, and the fight shifted further down the line, like a ball rolling downhill.

┼───═┼

Elements of Sumner's force had spread far enough south to clash with the forward center of the Confederate line, where D.H. Hill had his troops in a sunken road that zigzagged between two farms. The road became known as Bloody Lane because of the huge numbers of casualties who fell during the four-hour battle. Hill was using a musket himself, and Longstreet sent members of his personal staff to man an artillery piece. The Federal soldiers slowly seized the advantage, occupying Bloody Lane. They now needed only for the oncoming Union division of General Israel Richardson to punch through the thin, final defense line. But when Richardson fell, also mortally wounded, the entire attack on the center stalled.

┼───═┼

As pressure eased along his front, Jackson, who had not eaten all day, ravenously devoured some peaches. Now that his line had solidified, both he and Lee wanted to know if a counterattack might be launched. Jackson had an agile young soldier shinny up a tree and report on how many regimental battle standards could be seen. When the boy had counted to 39, even the aggressive Jackson had to decide against plunging into such a mass. His troops had taken a fearful beating through the morning. Even if he had wanted to counterattack, he would have been hard pressed to find enough unmangled units to carry out the order.

┼───═┼

McClellan shifted his attention to the Confederate right flank and the bridge across Antietam Creek. The task of capturing the bridge was given to the balding Major General Ambrose E. Burnside, whose eloquent whiskers, which looped from his ears to his mustache, inspired the term "sideburns" for men's facial hair.

If Burnside could take the bridge, then Union troops could cross and attack Sharpsburg itself. But Burnside fed in his four divisions one at a time rather than in concert, funneling them onto the narrow bridge, where some 400 Georgia troops mowed them down as they came. The Georgians held the narrow bridge for more than three hours.

It was about one o'clock in the afternoon before the bridge was taken. Burnside had turned the Confederate right flank, and the way into Sharpsburg now lay open. But the battle had taken too long. After being held up for so long at the bridge, Burnside then squandered two more hours in getting his men over the water and into position to advance up the ridge toward town. It was the final Federal mistake of a long day of mistakes.

✦━━✦

Jackson's last division saved the day. A.P. Hill had wrapped things up in Harper's Ferry, and his first units started the 17-mile march up to Sharpsburg as the sunlight began to fade. They pitched into Burnside's exposed flank and drove him back to some high ground near the bridge, where he remained.

The Battle of Antietam, only a single day of fighting, ended with some 23,000 total casualties. The Union army lost 2,108 killed, 9,549 wounded, and 753 captured or missing. The Confederates sustained 1,512 dead, 7,816 wounded, and 1,844 captured or missing. The U.S. National Park Service states that "Antietam resulted in nine times as many Americans killed or wounded as took place on June 6, 1944—D-day, the so-called 'longest day' of World War II. Also consider that more soldiers were killed and wounded at the Battle of Antietam than the deaths of all Americans in the Revolutionary War, War of 1812, Mexican War, and Spanish-American War combined." [4]

CHAPTER 19

Three Stars

THE REBEL ARMY WAS IN EXTREME DANGER ON THE NIGHT FOL-
lowing the horror of Antietam. The Potomac River was at their backs, and to
their front were thousands of Federal soldiers. The Union held all of the
strategic points—the East, West, and North Woods, Miller's shorn cornfield,
the Bloody Lane, Burnside's Bridge, and the fords across Antietam Creek. A
third of Lee's army had been lost, and if the enemy launched aggressive new
attacks, the consequences were sure to be disastrous.

But George McClellan's Union army had also suffered greatly, losing
about a fourth of its number, and he knew that the Confederate line remained tight and solid despite its shrunken size. Trying to smash through
would be costly. He still thought he did not have enough men and declined
to strike what might have been the ultimate blow of the war.

The exhausted legions watched each other warily throughout the following day, September 18, and when the second night came, Lee's army limped
down to the Potomac and began the escape into Virginia. In hindsight,

Antietam was clearly a fight that Lee should not have chosen, for it corralled him into a defensive slugfest that prevented maneuver everywhere except along his interior lines. Nevertheless, there was no reason for the South to believe McClellan would command this fight any better than he had the previous ones. The errant general's orders gave McClellan an extraordinary advantage, but he still was not up to the task. Jackson assured Lee afterward that the fight had been worth it. The outcome put the Confederates back on their own soil in Virginia.

+━━━+

A Confederate artillery officer covering the withdrawal panicked and allowed Union infantry to cross the Potomac. Before Lee even learned of the threat, Stonewall Jackson had A.P. Hill's relatively fresh division rushing to the endangered area. A vicious counterattack drove the Northern soldiers back into the river, where they were slaughtered trying to wade back to the Maryland shore. Hundreds of blue-clad bodies washed downstream.

Even during that final fight, the main body of the Southern army moved on and entered the welcoming arms of Winchester. Wounded men quickly filled the homes and buildings, leaving more to sit in the streets and await help. The invasion of Maryland had depleted the army, and each man who fell represented a severe loss, since the pool from which to draw replacements by now seemed almost empty. Only a trickle of volunteers had stepped forward in Maryland, and the casualties were amplified by the sick, stragglers, deserters, and soldiers refusing to be part of an invading army. At Winchester, Lee could count only about 36,000 men, including Jackson's shrunken command of less than 11,000 at a camp five miles north of Winchester.

+━━━+

Antietam was still a fresh wound when Abraham Lincoln solved the South's manpower problem by issuing the Emancipation Proclamation. The war would no longer be only about preserving the Union, but also about freeing enslaved black people. The prospect of Negroes being set loose ignited a blaze of anger and fear throughout the South. Experienced soldiers returned to duty, and from Mississippi to Virginia, men and boys surged forward to join the Confederate ranks.

Jackson soon would be able to count upward of 25,000 soldiers, and more were coming in every day. Their training was conducted by hardened veterans of many campaigns.

<hr />

By any normal measure, George McClellan won at Antietam, in that his enemy left the field. But Lincoln viewed the "victory" as hollow, for McClellan had promised to destroy Lee and again failed to do so, even with the Confederate battle plan spread before him. Antietam only restored balance. The Rebels were back on their home ground, the Stars and Bars still flew over Richmond, and McClellan was cowering around Washington with a huge Federal army. Two weeks after the battle, Lincoln personally directed him to advance. McClellan agreed, and proceeded to stay put.

One can only imagine the chagrin at the White House a short time later when pesky Confederate cavalryman Jeb Stuart, who had ridden around McClellan's entire army down in Virginia, did it again. This time, Stuart's troopers raided into Pennsylvania and came out through Maryland with taunting ease, losing just a single man killed and only a few wounded or drunk on Yankee whiskey. That was not the act of a beaten army.

After reporting to Lee that McClellan was anchored in place, Stuart galloped over to see his friend Jackson, who was delighted by the daring, unexpected, and deceptive raid. Movement was what he was all about. When he saw Stuart, Stonewall hooted in welcome, "How do you do, Pennsylvania?" [1]

Lincoln wanted generals like that! He was tired of strutting peacocks whose results did not match their words. At the end of October, he packed General Don Carlos Buell into retirement from the Army of the Ohio for failures in the Tennessee-Kentucky theater. Then he again fired McClellan, who was always slow, always blaming others, always wanting more—a general better in politics than in combat.

McClellan had waited until October 26 before petulantly crossing the Potomac almost by inches, thus wasting the best marching weather of the season. He concentrated the army around Warrenton, at the eastern end of the Blue Ridge Mountains, and as usual, stopped. Lincoln removed him from command in the first week of November. He was given a farewell ovation by the Army of the Potomac, which cherished him. The pompous general had one more fight to lose. Two years later he ran as the Democratic candidate for president and was trounced by Abraham Lincoln.

+>===≪+

McClellan's refusal to engage allowed Robert E. Lee the precious gift of time—several months worth in which to rest, recuperate, train, and rearm. He responded to the Union buildup around Warrenton by once again splitting his army, this time leaving a yawning gap of 175 miles between the two halves. General Longstreet shifted to Culpeper, 20 miles in front of Warrenton, to block any thrust against Richmond.

Stonewall Jackson stayed at the mouth of the Shenandoah, where he was allowed to do as he saw fit with his independent command, and maintained distant contact with Longstreet. Even while rebuilding and training, Jackson did not leave his troops idle. The whole point of his position was to stop the Union from venturing from Harper's Ferry, which the Rebels had abandoned when it ceased to be of use. Several Federal probes were discovered and driven back. Miles and miles of railroad track were destroyed by Jackson's men. They built bonfires with the wooden cross-ties, heated the steel rails, and bent them like pretzels. Jackson threw one division to the southern side of the Blue Ridge Mountains to cause mischief over there.

+>===≪+

Admiration for Jackson arced like a rainbow of hope all over Dixie. It was more than popularity, it was true fame, a stature exceeded only by the open love people held for Robert E. Lee. A Georgia soldier reported hearing cheers down the road one day, and someone remarked that it had to be either Stonewall Jackson or a rabbit. "Everyone made for the road and sure enough, it was Gen. Jackson galloping along the road with his escort. He passed us with his cap off and the cheering continued down the line as far as we could hear."[2]

Despite the heavy casualties his units incurred in battle, they knew he was not a heartless warrior. He spoke courteously with common soldiers, was deeply religious, and displayed great tenderness with women and small children. One of the most lingering examples of his nature came when a young mother begged the general to bless her baby. Jackson, in the saddle, gathered the 18-month-old child in his arms and held it so close that his long beard brushed the infant's hair. His staff members doffed their hats as the general closed his eyes and spent a time in silent prayer while the thankful mother leaned for support against the solid shoulder of Little Sorrel.

The touching moment may have been related to Jackson's knowledge that he was about to become a father himself, though none of his men were aware of this. Anna was pregnant. The child had been conceived during her stay with Jackson in Winchester.

<hr />

Jackson tried to wring all he could from the golden respite of October and November, for he not only had to get his troops into fighting trim but also to catch up on months of paperwork and personnel decisions. He was far behind on writing the official reports of his battles, and although he preferred biblical brevity—short, clear accounts that gave all credit for victory to God—the Confederate government wanted military-style detail. In the end, he hired an attorney who had served in Congress to conduct the needed interviews and catch up on the writing.

He strongly supported the religious revival that swept through the Second Corps, as ministers thronged to the campsites to preach the Gospel. Jackson frequently joined his soldiers in prayer, and many soldiers came to the revivals just because he did. He attended formal church services whenever he could, although he usually slept through the sermons.

His personnel decisions were based on criteria known only to him. He created a storm of protest by filling the vacant command of the Stonewall Brigade with Major Frank "Bull" Paxton, a mid-level officer on his staff, a fellow Presbyterian, and a personal friend. The job came with the star of a brigadier general, three grades above Paxton's present rank. The appointment pushed aside the acting commander, popular Colonel Andrew Jackson Grigsby of the 27th Virginia Regiment, who had stepped forward to control an entire division during Antietam. Jackson did not approve of some of Grigsby's personal habits, so the fearless and battle-hardened field commander resigned and returned home to Lexington, depriving the army of a strong sword at a critical time.

The single most bedeviling thing for Jackson at the time was his ongoing personal feud with the prickly A.P. Hill, who still held his grudge about being arrested even after he and Jackson had fought together flawlessly. When calm descended, Hill wrote to Lee to "deny the truth of every allegation" made against him and to demand a court of inquiry. He told Jeb Stuart that his reputation had been damaged by "that crazy old Presbyterian."

Lee wanted the clash between two of his most valuable combat leaders just to go away, and Jackson was willing to drop it as well. Like it or not, his most vocal critic was also his second-in-command, both in seniority and courage. Jackson and Lee were satisfied that Hill had taken to heart the reprimand for not adhering strictly to orders. However, no two officers in the entire Confederate army were more stubborn than Stonewall Jackson and A.P. Hill, and when Hill continued to complain, Jackson responded in kind, causing the feud to escalate every further. Lee chose to let time pass without doing anything, and the two men remained stiffly formal with each other when not fighting side by side.

Hill knew he would never overturn Stonewall's pedestal. He grumbled that even if Jackson someday got "the damnedest thrashing . . . I should get my share and probably all the blame, for the people will never blame Stonewall for any disaster." [3]

<hr />

By November, Lee's army numbered about 85,000 men, and he restructured it into a pair of corps.

The three-star rank of lieutenant general was bestowed upon James Longstreet, who was assigned to command the First Corps, with 45,000 troops. Stonewall Jackson was given his third star a day behind Longstreet on the seniority list and assumed command of the Second Corps, almost 40,000 soldiers. His divisional leaders were formidable: both Hills, Jubal Early, and William Taliaferro, who had recovered from his wound at Second Bull Run.

Jeb Stuart gave Jackson a uniform jacket custom-made by a Richmond tailor and more suitable for a lieutenant general than the faded old VMI tunic, whose buttons had all gone to ladies demanding them as precious trophies. Stonewall donned the fine costume for a dinner with his staff, expressing appreciation of Stuart's gesture but also declaring that the coat was too fine for him; he did not wear it again for several months. When his higher pay grade took effect, Jackson increased the tithe to his church in Lexington.

All of the personal adulation embarrassed Jackson, particularly the gifts that deluged his headquarters, everything from new clothes to a fancy captured sword. While the presents poured in, he was trying to obtain supplies and equipment for his troops before the onset of winter. They needed everything, and the official channels were proving inadequate to the task of supplying them. Residents of the Valley gave what they could, with people back home sending their boys equipment and clothes. But when the first chill winds penetrated the mountains, thousands of soldiers still had no overcoats, gloves, blankets, and shoes. And there would be no building of log huts and sturdy lean-tos for winter quarters around Winchester, for the time was fast approaching for the troops to march again.

Across the way, Major General Ambrose Burnside had replaced his good friend George McClellan at the top of the Army of the Potomac. He was quite unsure of himself, and that lack of confidence filtered down from his headquarters.

Robert E. Lee could almost smell the pressure coming from Washington on the new Union commander to do something. Lee just didn't know what. He sent word to Jackson that the enemy was edging southward and that Stonewall should be prepared to close the gap between the two Confederate corps. It was merely a suggestion, not a direct order.

Burnside also knew that Lincoln demanded action so, despite his timidity, he quickly took unprecedented steps. He had 120,000 men and plenty of reserves and supplies. He altered the structure into three "Grand Divisions"—each containing several corps—and in a reversal of tactics, got them moving so quickly that the Confederates lost sight of them. Burnside went southeast down the Rappahannock toward the riverfront town of Fredericksburg, only 50 miles from Richmond.

The beautifully executed maneuver achieved surprise, and was a successful first step in what promised to be a handsome strike. The second part of the plan was to have army engineers advance near the front elements to swiftly throw pontoon bridges across the Rappahannock. His troops would then capture Fredericksburg before the Rebs could react. The bridges were so critical that Burnside had given the task to General-in-Chief Halleck in Washington, who would have the ability to override all obstacles and push the orders through.

On November 17, the residents of Fredericksburg and a handful of Confederate soldiers looked across the river with astonishment. Column after column of blue uniforms snaked through the towns of Falmouth and Chatham just to the northeast, and the Yankee army grabbed Stafford Heights, the dominating geographical feature on the east side of the Rappahannock. They would put artillery up there and be ready to cross as soon as the portable bridges were assembled. But there were no pontoon bridges. Nobody knew where they were.

Now it was the turn of the Union soldiers on the eastern bank to spend day after day watching, as General Longstreet came down the other side of the river and spread his 45,000 troops along the western ridges that overlooked Fredericksburg. Burnside had lost the chance for a quick victory.

<hr/>

Snow was falling in the Valley, and the early winter chewed at Jackson's Second Corps. Barefoot men tied strips of cowhide around their feet, only to have it tighten miserably when the leather was soaked by melting snow and ice. The major sources of warmth for many were just working up a sweat during the day and huddling around a campfire at night.

Jackson heard a Rebel yell erupt in the camp one night, spreading until the entire area was swept up in a raucous war-whoop. Stonewall listened to the roar and commented, "That was the sweetest music I ever heard."[4] They were cold and miserable, but the morale was high. They were ready to fight.

He decided that he had waited long enough, and Second Corps began the 175-mile journey to Fredericksburg, one step at a time. Jackson's trademark tactic was his ability to shift positions in a hurry to get his troops to where they were most needed, usually without the enemy realizing he was even on the move.

Jackson's men tramped away down the turnpike, leaving just enough troops behind to dispel any notion the Union might have of attacking Winchester. His decision to head toward Fredericksburg was unknown even to General Lee, who wrote him the following day with the suggestion "to move east of the Blue Ridge." Jackson was already on the way.

They trekked south in bitter cold, retracing routes over familiar territory such as Kernstown and around Massanutten Mountain, through the gap into the Luray Valley, on into the Blue Ridge and through Thornton's Gap before spilling onto the flat Piedmont. They were out of the mountains, but rain, sleet, and snow lashed their faces and soaked their clothes. Each morning began with freezing temperatures, but the pitiful foot cavalry somehow pulled themselves together each day and stomped on for more miles, with rocks and sharp ice cutting into their bare feet.

⊣≡≡⊢

During a brief bivouac around Gordonsville, Jackson received a note from Harriet Irwin, Anna's sister, notifying him that Anna had given birth to a baby girl at Harriet's home in Charlotte, North Carolina, on November 23. The general was overcome with joy and thanksgiving that both mother and their blue-eyed, dark-haired, eight-and-one-half pound daughter were healthy, and he sank to his knees in private prayer. With typical secrecy, he had insisted on being notified of the birth by personal message and not telegram, which would have been faster but also would have been read by others. He did not share the good news with his staff.

Later, a letter arrived. "Aunt Harriet says I am the express image of my darling papa," read the note that Harriet had penned as if had been written by the baby. Although he wanted a boy, Jackson responded that the child should be told that her father "loves her better than all the baby-boys in the world, and better than all the other babies in the world." [5] He named her Julia, after his mother; for Christmas, he would receive a lock of her hair.

The birth of his child energized Stonewall Jackson, and soldiers noticed that he began riding Little Sorrel with his back erect like a proud horseman at the head of his corps. He took four couriers and a staff member and struck out for a fast 40-mile ride to where Lee had established his headquarters. At dusk, the long route took them through a dismal tangle of dense woods and past a brick tavern on an intersection, where the battles of the Wilderness and Chancellorsville would later be fought. Rain was falling on civilian refugees from Fredericksburg, and Jackson carefully wove his way through them. Finally, he found Mine Road, and Robert E. Lee emerged from his headquarters tent to greet him. Jackson spent the night in a warm bed, indoors.

On the final Sunday of November, Stonewall Jackson trotted the final five miles into the empty city of Fredericksburg, pulled Little Sorrel to a halt at a snowy intersection, and just sat silently for a while. Neither he nor Lee wanted to fight at Fredericksburg, both preferring to swing onto the offensive. Stonewall observed that after beating the Yankees, the Rebel army would be unable to pursue across the Rappahannock and crush them because of the Federal artillery on Stafford Heights. Instead, he wanted to fight along the North Anna River, 30 miles to the south, where they would be able to maneuver. That would mean giving up both Fredericksburg and 30 miles of precious Virginia ground, and Lee knew this would have a demoralizing impact on the entire South. The politicians wouldn't stand for it.

With the North Anna not an option, the battle had to be fought at Fredericksburg, where Jackson saw almost perfect defensive positions for the Confederates. If the Yankees chose to fight there, they also would have no fruits of victory. He was sure they couldn't win.

CHAPTER 20

Fredericksburg

AMBROSE BURNSIDE WAS UNABLE TO ADAPT TO THE CHANGED conditions. Instead of trying to exploit another river crossing point when the pontoon bridges did not arrive on time, he allowed his powerful army to grind to a halt. By the time he finally got around to attacking, Stonewall Jackson had arrived from more than a hundred miles away, and Lee's entire army was ready. "I fear they will continue to make these changes until they find someone whom I don't understand," mused Lee. [1]

Fredericksburg was a city of precise dimensions laid out like a checkerboard on the west side of the Rappahannock, which was about 400 feet wide where it swept past the city, north to south. Directly behind the town rose Marye's Heights, a thick ridge named after the family that owned the white-columned manor house that crowned it. Along the forward edge of the ridge was a road worn down by traffic lower than the surrounding ground and bordered by a solid fence of large rocks.

Longstreet's troops were entrenched on the high, heavily wooded ground, with multiple ranks of infantry behind the wall and guarded by files of big guns. Having been given an extraordinary amount of time to plot the ground, his artillery chief promised that not even a chicken could get through the crossfire he had laid out over the low approaches up from the river and the edge of town.

To the south, the ground flattened into more open country, providing room for an attacking force to gather, although still rising away from the river bank to the wooded ridge. The Confederate line thinned considerably beyond that.

Lee thought Burnside would make a downstream crossing rather than charge into the teeth of Longstreet's obvious strength. Therefore, John Bell Hood's Texans extended the right of the line, and Stonewall Jackson's Second Corps linked beyond that in a thin shield for some 20 miles.

Jackson had built his line throughout the first week of December as the units arrived from the long march. The six-brigade division of his disagreeable partner, Major General A.P. Hill, was stationed nearest the Texans. Taliaferro's Stonewall Division spread several more miles further downstream, where they joined Jubal Early's division around Skinker's Neck. D.H. Hill took over from there, with Jeb Stuart roaming the final area of the right flank all the way to the river at Port Royal.

⊬━━⊣

Burnside seemed jinxed. His life was filled with opportunity but not accomplishment: He had missed action in the Mexican War; he was unable to take a new cavalry carbine he invented into production; his fiancé abandoned him on their wedding day. Somehow, though, the tall soldier maintained an infectious kindness toward all. He had told Lincoln that he was "not competent to command such a large army as this," and was proving that prediction accurate.

Having given the Confederates every opportunity to move into place at their leisure, Burnside unveiled his final plan on December 10. Senior officers let him know they believed it was a recipe for doom, and their lack of optimism seeped out to the troops, who would have to cross the river and parade over open ground before even trying to climb the ridges to dig out the waiting Rebels. The men could see what lay beyond the water.

Burnside was running out of options. After the bold opening gambit to reach Fredericksburg, he could not retreat. With Stonewall Jackson in position downriver, and the level of potential fording points raised by days of rain, a swinging flank attack was out of the question. He *had* to fight at this place, and the pontoons and timbers had finally arrived.

Long before the chilly, foggy dawn of December 11, Union engineers started throwing bridges across the Rappahannock. The first spans were to be laid just north of the city. With Union artillery studding Stafford Heights, Confederate infantry formations were unable to occupy the shoreline, but the brick walls of the waterfront buildings and homes in Fredericksburg were perfect nests for the 1,600 sharpshooters and snipers of a Mississippi brigade. They opened fire on the engineers and repeatedly drove them back to cover. Without the bridges, the "Grand Division" of General Sumner remained stuck on the eastern shore. Burnside finally let his cannon smash Fredericksburg to rubble with thousands of rounds. Landing parties used the pontoons as boats to establish and protect a bridgehead and chase the stubborn snipers from their hiding holes. The Mississippi marksmen had set the Union timetable back by an entire day.

Lacking a position that could deter the crossing and preferring to keep his troops out of view, Jackson let the enemy come over the water. He watched Union engineers complete their bridges and the soldiers cross unopposed. Thousands of men from the Grand Division of General William B. Franklin formed ranks on the flat, solid ground. There they stopped for the night.

The Confederate generals knew exactly where the fighting would come, and Lee decided to tighten the Longstreet position behind Fredericksburg and to shift Hood's Texas division even nearer. Jackson pulled A.P. Hill over to close upon the new front line. More guns would cover the same dirt.

Jackson awoke at four o'clock on December 12, ate breakfast in weather that was still below freezing, and rode away alone to reconnoiter the lines.

Hill's troops were tied with the Texas men all the way down to the dominating high ground of Prospect Hill some two miles downriver. Jackson,
always looking for ways to deceive and baffle the enemy, left only a picket
line hidden behind a railroad embankment, while his big brigades disappeared into the thick stand of woods behind it. The artillery was also kept
out of sight.

The only empty gap was a tangled bog that descended into a ravine between two brigades on the left. It was half a mile wide and extended more
than 600 yards into the Rebel lines. It is unclear whether Jackson was aware
of the unguarded section, but it would have been very unusual for him not
to have perceived the advantages and weaknesses of every point on his line.
He was so satisfied with the overall positions that he was actually heard
whistling. Historians generally agree that almost everyone knew of the exposed tongue of land. But with so many artillery pieces and infantrymen
covering the approaches, and with other Rebel troops in the rear, the
swampy gap did not get the attention it deserved.

As the Union lines formed, Lee and Jackson walked together to within
about 400 yards of them for a better look. It was clear that Burnside had
abandoned any idea of crossing the Rappahannock downriver and would
strike across the ground on which the two generals were standing. Jackson
summoned the rest of the foot cavalry from their distant positions. Instead
of having to defend an extraordinarily long and narrow front, he would be
able to consolidate into a beefy defense-in-depth directly before the Federal
strength.

Unmolested, Jackson was able to maneuver into a virtually unassailable
position. No longer worried about his right flank, he left only two brigades
of Jeb Stuart's horsemen and artillery as a blocking force at that end. The immense power of Hood and Longstreet covered his left. In a stark reversal of
his own penchant for swooping around to find an enemy weak point, Jackson now positioned his units as an anvil at the point where the enemy would
have to strike.

Behind A.P. Hill, the divisions of Taliaferro and Jubal Early formed another line of defense along the wooded ridge. D.H. Hill would be layered in
a third line, behind Early and in front of Prospect Hill, since the highest
ground probably would be a primary target of the Union attack. A road in
the woods provided a safe alley in which the troops could move quickly. In-

stead of covering the original 20 miles, the Second Corps had been compressed into a combined arms defense only two miles long—and a mile deep! Artillery, infantry and cavalry stood ready to fight, mostly hidden and unseen by the enemy. Every big gun was sited.

+━━ ━━+

Before dawn the following morning, Saturday, December 13, heavy fog was cushioned against the ground, creating a haze made even thicker by smoke from the burning buildings of Fredericksburg and thousands of campfires.

Jackson decided to change his appearance for the coming battle. The tattered VMI kepi and tunic and even Little Sorrel were left behind that morning. He rode out on a proud stallion, looking every inch a Confederate lieutenant general in his new gold-trimmed uniform. His new look surprised the soldiers, but when they realized it was just Old Jack beneath all that finery, loud whoops of approval erupted, although some grumbled that it just didn't look right for him to be so dressed up.

Arriving at Lee's hilltop headquarters, Jackson blushed at the compliments, and then demonstrated that the new clothes had not changed the inner man. His aggressiveness flashed as he declared his desire to attack the Yankees before the fog lifted and push them back into the water, but he was refused. Lee decided this day would be one for defense first, with a counterattack possible later. As the mist lifted, Jackson and the others saw Yankees gathered as thick as fleas along the western side of the Rappahannock.

It had taken two days for all of Franklin's infantry, cavalry, and artillery—some 27,000 men—to get over the river on Jackson's front. An equal number under General Sumner gathered around Fredericksburg and thoroughly looted the town. General Joe Hooker's Grand Division of 30,000 men spread between the two wings, with orders to be available to support the other attacks. The blue lines began to stir.

Longstreet teased Jackson. "General, do not all those multitudes of Federals frighten you?"

"We shall very soon see whether I shall not frighten them!" Jackson retorted.[2]

—⊨═══⊨—

By nine o'clock, Stonewall was checking his artillery positions and riding among the thick ranks of soldiers, his blue eyes bright in anticipation of a successful battle. Yankee cannoneers across the river began searching for the Rebels concealed in the woods. Trees blew apart, splinters flying and limbs falling, and the Union battle lines started forward. An officer voiced concern to Jackson, who snapped back, "Major, my men have sometimes failed to *take* a position, but to *defend* one, never!" [3]

—⊨═══⊨—

With a galaxy of troops at his disposal, Franklin gave the critical job of attacking Jackson to his smallest division, the 5,000 Pennsylvania soldiers of Major General George B. Meade. Born in Spain, Meade was a lackadaisical cadet at West Point with strong Southern connections in his family, and he had to pull every string he could find to win a brigadier general's commission. Very aggressive by nature, he detested the hesitation of McClellan and Burnside and believed Franklin to be just as cautious. A genius in field engineering, he took one look at the topography and knew the advantage lay with Jackson.

Meade started his troops forward across the open ground in three long battle lines about ten o'clock. Their bright regimental colors, the martial measures of drums and bugles, and a warming sun gave the movement the look of a holiday demonstration. Major General John Gibbon was to move on his right flank, with Major General Abner Doubleday on the left, at the end of the Federal line.

Union artillery covered the advance, but Jackson kept his own big guns silent and hidden. Young Major John Pelham of Alabama, accustomed to being very mobile as the leader of Stuart's horse artillery, was allowed to rush out on the flank of the advancing Federals around two o'clock. The major unlimbered a single 12-pound Napoleon artillery piece and blasted the Yankees in enfilade. A second cannon crew galloped up to join the attack, and the pair tore great, bloody holes in the lines of the Union soldiers moving across their front like ducks in a shooting gallery. The crews moved frequently, but Union artillery managed to destroy one of the Confederate guns. Pelham ignored orders to withdraw and continued to do extraordinary damage. Only when he ran out of ammunition did he hook up his gun and return to the main lines. His flank assault, which had been watched closely and admired by Robert E. Lee himself, brought the day's first Federal advance to a cold stop.

+>==<+

The Union guns then opened up with a vengeance, but the Rebels remained invisible and quiet. When the hour-long barrage lifted, the Northern infantry moved forward again, but Gibbon lagged well behind the pace of Meade. Doubleday stayed in place on the far left to prevent another surprise from Jeb Stuart's roving artillerymen. That left Meade's men practically on their own.

Jackson had traded the big showy stallion for his battle-tested friend Little Sorrel, and both seemed totally unconcerned about the explosions all around them. When he rode forward with an aide for a better look, a Yankee bullet passed right between the two men. Both left the field safely, and Jackson lay down comfortably on his back while waiting for the Yankee attack to unfold. Rifle fire buzzed above him. His entire corps was holding its breath, waiting for the order to engage, but Stonewall held them in check to let the enemy drift into targets that could not be missed.

He gave the approval to fire at about noon, when the Yankees were only about 800 yards away. A salvo from more than 50 hidden Rebel artillery pieces crashed into the blue formation, which sagged apart, regrouped, and came forward again, only to have the bloody process repeated. Then they ran into withering fire from the waiting Rebel infantry. "Come on, blue-bellies, we want them blankets!" yelled one Rebel rifleman. Another taunted, "Take off them boots!" Still another called out, "Bring them rations along! You've got to leave them!" [4]

The desperate Union soldiers made for the only apparent place of safety, the open gap in A.P. Hill's line. With artillery and infantry fire tearing at them, they plunged into the thick woods of the little valley, and more Federal troops poured in behind them like water rushing toward a drain. Incredibly, Meade's battered troops broke through Stonewall Jackson's line. They swept past the brigades flanking the swamp and, by running forward and crowding in, expanded the opening.

It was just when the defense-in-depth tactic was supposed to click into place, for the Confederate brigade of General Maxcy Gregg was in reserve at the head of the gap. But Gregg was caught so unprepared that his men were relaxing with their weapons stacked when Union soldiers burst into their ranks. Gregg fell with a bullet in the spine. As would be demonstrated in future wars, particularly in Iraq, commanders behind the front lines must remain as alert as those doing the shooting.

Jackson was not overly concerned. Jubal Early rushed his division toward the fighting, while Jackson himself brought over elements of D.H. Hill's division. The influx of blue-clad soldiers was stopped and the hole plugged violently when Early slammed onto the intruders with seven brigades and the Rebel units on the sides of the swamp pounded the flanks. The advantage turned into a three-sided ambush because of a lack of Union support. The following retreat became a rout, and the Federals were flushed from the wooded sanctuary back into the open field, where they were scythed again by the artillery and infantry before reaching the safety of the main Union lines.

Near Prospect Hill, Jackson brought Little Sorrel to a halt, raised his hand to the heavens, and lowered his head in prayer. The big guns thundered on, but the infantry fight was over in his sector. Stonewall Jackson was victorious again.

+>===+

As badly as the battle had gone on the left side of the Union line, things got worse when it shifted to Fredericksburg during the afternoon. Repeated frontal assaults uphill into the powerful Longstreet positions ended in massacre. No Union soldier got within 100 feet of the stone wall. Burnside made the same mistake as McClellan at Antietam, feeding in his overwhelming force a piece at a time, allowing each to be independently butchered by a stout Rebel defense. Only the butchering in Fredericksburg was one-sided. "It is well that this is so terrible!" said Robert E. Lee as he watched the slaughter and realized victory was in his grasp. "We should grow too fond of it!"[5]

Jackson decided to counterattack at sunset, but his orders to the division commanders were either late or confusing, if they arrived at all, and the Union artillery on Stafford Heights pounded the Confederate guns the moment they tried to lay down a preparatory barrage. His corps had already suffered 344 men killed that day and 2,545 wounded, with another 526 missing. He had predicted that attacking across the treacherous ground controlled by enemy artillery would not be successful, and the big guns thundering unabated from across the river persuaded him to call it off.

+>===<+

It took a long time for Jackson to settle down from the day's excitement. A friend showed up from Richmond with fresh oysters for dinner. The general wanted little sleep, toiling through much of the night with paperwork and paying a personal visit to the badly wounded Maxcy Gregg, easing Gregg's mind about their past personal differences and holding the hand of the dying officer.

Outside on the battlefield, temperatures plummeted and mangled wounded men cried for help among the piles of frozen dead bodies. No one could venture into the zone, which was still under fire.

Burnside was expected to resume the attack at daylight. Hunter McGuire, Jackson's personal physician and friend, reported to him as the sun came up that immense Federal forces remained on the field. He asked Jackson what he intended to do, and Stonewall savagely replied, "Kill them, sir! Kill every one."[6]

There was some skirmishing that day, but no full attacks. Union officers asked Jackson for a truce that afternoon to attend to their dead and wounded. Jackson refused until Burnside personally signed the request. As his own rescue and medical units moved forward, he warned them not to reveal to the enemy that he was in command of the sector. It was an unnecessary order, for the Union soldiers already knew the secret.

Heavy weather, hard rain, and crackling winds moved in at dark. When the fog evaporated the next morning, there were no Union troops on either side of the Rappahannock River around Fredericksburg.

CHAPTER 21

Final Fight

With major fighting in Virginia done for the bloody year of 1862, Stonewall Jackson settled into winter quarters a dozen miles below Fredericksburg on the grounds of a large mansion known as Moss Neck. The beautiful home was owned by Richard Corbin, a gentleman planter serving as a private in Stonewall's command. Corbin and his wife urged Jackson to stay in the main building, but the general declined, concerned that he would violate the family's privacy. Instead, he would occupy a two-story hunting lodge about 500 yards from the house. That small place became the beating heart of the Second Corps for the next three months.

There was no Union threat against him. Lincoln shuffled Burnside off to the rubbish pile of Union generals who had been ruined in Virginia and, with great personal reservations, gave the job to tall, handsome, controversial Joe Hooker, who loved taverns and the ladies. "Fighting Joe" reorganized the Army of the Potomac once again, replacing the three "Grand Divisions" with seven infantry and a full cavalry corps. His strong points were building morale, organizing, and training. His weakness was losing his determination when the stakes were the highest.

After Fredericksburg, pickets from both armies dug "gopher holes" along the Rappahannock banks and watched each other as they shivered in the cold. Having seen the effectiveness of the defense along the sunken road and wall at Fredericksburg, the Rebel commanders spent much of the winter creating a virtually impregnable system of ditches and breastworks along the advantageous ground. The advantage was clear: a rifleman in a hole is protected from direct cannon and rifle fire and can therefore survive and fight longer. An entrenched platoon can stop a company. That lesson of Fredericksburg would impress itself so deeply in military minds that even today, almost all soldiers carry entrenching tools.

Life in Jackson's camp fell into routines, some pleasant and some harsh. Officers were entertained at various mansions. Troops staged plays and listened to regimental band concerts that ended with rousing renditions of "Dixie" and a chorus of rebel yells that rolled across the countryside. But thousands of soldiers left camp to visit their homes or deserted the army altogether. Courts-martial were commonplace.

+≻━━≺+

As usual in times of quiet, there was turmoil among Jackson's generals. His brother-in-law D.H. Hill departed as a divisional commander to lead the fight in North Carolina. Another experienced division leader, General Taliaferro, whom Jackson never forgave for siding with his opponent during the Romney controversy in the Valley, was denied promotion despite his proven combat record. Taliaferro furiously requested a transfer, which he received. A.P. Hill resumed the ongoing fight to clear his name. A brigadier general was brought up on charges of cowardice. Even a general's stars could not protect an officer from Stonewall's wrath. When he was in command, he was in total command.

+≻━━≺+

The main thing troubling Lieutenant General Thomas J. Jackson was the absence of his family. He was terribly homesick. It was not unusual for senior officers to get their troops squared away for the cold months, then take leave and visit home. Jackson remained steadfastly at his post, but his frequent letters to Anna are filled with longing: "I haven't seen my wife for nearly a year—my home in nearly two years, and have never seen our darling little daughter."

When he received a lock of his child's hair at Christmas, he wrote, "How I do want to see that precious baby!" Instead, he had to settle for mailing fatherly advice on how to raise her, not to let her "have that will of her own," and not to call her a "cherub," because such angelic creatures existed only in Heaven.[1]

To fill part of that empty space in his heart, he asked the Corbins to allow their six-year-old daughter, Janie, to come and play in his office in the afternoons after the day's work was done. Janie became a favorite visitor, and would always receive little gifts. The stern general, feared by so many men, once even cut the gold lace off of his fancy hat for the delighted child, who had become a surrogate daughter to him.

The wives of some other generals ventured forward to visit their husbands, but the weather would be too dangerous for baby Julia, who was sick with chicken pox, to make such a trip.

Jackson was only 38 years old and in his prime. He was known in the South, the North, and abroad, and he seemed invincible. An English visitor during this period wrote of the lieutenant general: "I expected to see an old, untidy man, and was most agreeably surprised and pleased with his appearance. He is tall, handsome and powerfully built, but thin. He has brown hair and a brown beard. His mouth expresses great determination. The lips are thin and compressed firmly together; his eyes are blue and dark, with keen and searching expression."[2]

In March, he shifted his headquarters from Moss Neck into tents at Hamilton's Crossing, six miles south of Fredericksburg. It had been his field headquarters during the battle four months earlier, and might have to serve that purpose again: warmer weather was approaching, which meant the war would soon resume.

━━━━━

Across the Rappahannock, Fighting Joe Hooker had built the Army of the Potomac to about 135,000 men, and it was now ready to go. He had improved

their living conditions dramatically, delivered their back pay, fed, and fur-
loughed them. In turn, morale soared and the Union men took boisterous
pride in their new commander, singing out:

"Joe Hooker is our leader,
He takes his whiskey strong!"[3]

Hooker reported to President Lincoln that he was ready to launch a new offensive. "My plans are perfect!" he crowed. "And when I start to carry them
out, may God have mercy on General Lee, for I will have none!"[4] Lincoln
must have winced at that, for he had heard it before from other generals.
Commanders should win first and brag later.

⊹⟫━⟪⊹

Jackson's relief at getting back under canvas was shaken by news that little
Janie Corbin and two of her visiting young cousins had died of scarlet fever
at Moss Neck. His soldiers built their coffins and the general wept without
shame, deciding that he would wait no longer to see his family.

His wife and child arrived in a rainstorm on April 20 aboard the mail
train from Richmond to the supply depot at Guinea Station, five miles
below Hamilton's Crossing. Jackson boarded the train and met his daughter.
Julia had just awakened from a nap and gave a bright smile to the large
bearded man whose face lit up as he stared at her in wonder. He did not
gather the infant in his arms until their covered carriage arrived at the plantation home of William Yerby, where he had taken temporary lodging. He
was captivated by the plump and rosy-faced baby, and took to swinging her
merrily before a mirror, calling out, "Now, Miss Jackson, look at yourself!
Isn't she a little *gem?*" [5]

Without neglecting his work, he hurried home each day to spend as
much time as he could with Anna and Julia. On most days, he would invite
some officers to dine, but what he really wanted was to be alone with his
wife and play with their little girl. The day the child turned five months old,
she was baptized by a minister in the parlor of the Yerby home.

A week and a day were all he had for joy. On April 28, the windows of
the house rattled with distant salvos of cannon fire to the north. The pre-

cious respite was done, and Stonewall Jackson had to return to his business of killing.

⊹≻═≺⊹

Hooker did not want a repeat of the failed Burnside frontal attacks at Fredericksburg, particularly since the Confederates had strengthened the place even more during the winter. The key to defeating them lay at the river crossings far northwest of the city, so he took a page from Lee's playbook and divided his immense army.

The opening phase unfolded with an unexpected dash for a Union commander. The new cavalry corps—10,000 troopers strong—were to move out of the encampment unseen and ride far beyond the Confederate left flank, cross the river, then swoop back down to raid supply depots and communication routes between Lee and Richmond. Commanding them was General George Stoneman, a former roommate of Jackson at West Point. They both were so taciturn by nature that their quarters were the quietest at the entire academy. "Celerity, audacity and resolution are everything in war," Hooker instructed Stoneman. "Let your watchword be fight, fight, fight!"[6]

⊹≻═≺⊹

Once the horse soldiers began to disrupt things behind the Rebel lines, another 50,000 Union troops would demonstrate directly before the formidable entrenchments at Fredericksburg to hold Lee in place. The bulk of the army would then strike out to the northwest, cross the Rappahannock at the upriver fords, and wheel back south. Lee would have to come out from the Fredericksburg fortress and fight in the open.

Timing was extremely fortunate for the northern commander, because Lee had about 54,000 men left. General Longstreet had been dispatched with several divisions, including Hood's rugged Texans, to face a Yankee threat 120 miles distant.

Hooker had an excellent plan. The only thing missing was the clear understanding that he did not control the area's volatile springtime weather and that he was up against Robert E. Lee and Stonewall Jackson.

It took several days for the Stoneman cavalry to make it up to the Warrenton Junction area along the Orange & Alexandria Railroad, and then the skies opened. Torrential rains sent the Rappahannock into a rage that made the planned crossing impossible. Ten thousand cavalrymen sat there for two weeks waiting for the waters to subside. Rebel sentries taunted them from across the river. Grazing stallions were as useless as a grounded warplane.

+≻═━≺+

After two weeks of bad weather, Hooker decided to pursue the rest of his plan and let the cavalry join in when it could. He sent two corps across the Rappahannock south of Fredericksburg on April 26. Lee and Jackson considered attacking them, but recognized it as a feint and stayed on the defense.

Then Hooker unleashed his main punch, dispatching three infantry corps off for Kelly's Ford, 25 miles northwest. To speed them along, wagons were left behind in favor of some 2,000 pack mules. Brushing aside light Confederate opposition, they crossed on April 29, split their columns for easier movement, and plunged southeast toward the Confederate stronghold. As they advanced, they uncovered more fords, which were subsequently used to bring in even more Union divisions.

The powerful right wing of the Union attack force reunited in a tangled area of swamps and gullies that was dense with scrub oak and pine and known appropriately as the Wilderness. Inside it was Chancellorsville, a large farmhouse and outbuildings where five roads joined. Once his troops were concentrated, Hooker rode in on a big white horse to lead them. He had executed a brilliant sweep, and he announced with pride, "Our enemy must ingloriously fly, or come out from behind his defenses and give us battle on our own ground, where certain destruction awaits him."[7]

+≻═━≺+

Lee and Jackson had no intention of dodging the fight. "No sir!" Stonewall Jackson snorted when someone suggested retreat. "We shall not fall back! We shall defeat them!"[8]

Lee had been kept abreast of the Yankee movements by Jeb Stuart's cavalrymen. Prisoners from the three Union corps that had crossed Kelly's Ford confirmed what had taken place, proving that the real threat was upriver. A single Rebel division on the far left of the line swung around and dug in some three miles from Chancellorsville. Lee and Jackson spent most of April 30 riding the ridge behind Fredericksburg, examining the positions of the enemy there. Lee then decided to split his numerically inferior force. Jubal Early was left in the Fredericksburg trenches facing a force with five times as many men as his 10,000, while Lee took everyone else out to attack the Yankees in the Wilderness. Jackson pulled the Second Corps in from the south. It was time to make the greatest march of his career.

Stonewall Jackson knew the value of time and he had his corps moving long before dawn on May 1. A morning mist hid them from the Yankee spotters floating in balloons and mounted in observation points on high ground across the river. The Union telegraph line linking them to headquarters was out of order.

The missing Federal cavalry corps would now play an important role through its absence. Only a brigade of horse troopers had been held back as scouts, leaving Hooker blind to his enemy's tactical movements. The Union infantry commanders gathered at Chancellorsville wondered why they had not been ordered to advance in the bright moonlight, since only a single Confederate division seemed to be in front of them. Daylight came, but not the expected order to move out. Hooker, having accomplished a masterful job in getting into position, was hesitating. Unlike Jackson, he was wasting valuable hours. The needed order to move did not come until late in the morning.

By then, Jackson had scooped up the division that had dug in as an emergency defensive screen, and was advancing so confidently that it seemed that he, not Hooker, held the numerical advantage. The opposing forces slammed together at ten thirty in the morning, and the first battles of Chancellorsville exploded with extraordinary ferocity. Union and Confederate battle lines slashed at each other for two hours with neither side making a breakthrough.

Joe Hooker was the first to blink. Fearful that some of his units might be surrounded, he ordered them all to retreat back to the day's original positions. The order shocked many of his commanders, who had to give up hard-won ground. As the Union soldiers built a strong position in the woods that night, a spirit of defeatism settled upon them. They did not know why, but it was obvious that somehow they had been flipped onto the defensive. "The high expectations which had animated them only a few hours ago had given place to disappointment," said General Darius Nash Couch, a corps commander under Hooker and another former Jackson West Point classmate. [9] They found it hard to accept Hooker's bland explanation that the plan now was to lure the Rebels into making frontal attacks and impaling themselves on the Union strongpoint.

+≻═≺+

Daylight gave out early in the Wilderness, as Jackson and Lee discussed strategy and wondered why Hooker had come to a halt. Hooker might have lacked adequate cavalry scouts, but the Rebels had some of the best eyes in the business. When Jeb Stuart came in with a surprising report, it all fell into place. Rebel cavalry was free to roam because the Yankee cavalry corps was still behind the high waters and would not influence the battle. Even better news was that the Union XI Corps at the western end of the line had become separated from the main body at Chancellorsville.

Stuart's information galvanized the two supremely aggressive leaders. They studied maps, examined reports of enemy strength, and interviewed a minister familiar with roads in the area, looking for some way to work a bold attack. Jackson made sure to get some sleep, and so did Lee. Stonewall was up first, huddled in the chill beside a campfire. He was sniffling, catching a cold. Before dawn, around four o'clock, Lee joined him. As they sat on boxes of hardtack biscuits discarded by the Union soldiers, Jackson's trusted map man, Jed Hotchkiss, laid the scene before them. They had found a wide road used by woodcutters, ten miles long and big enough for horses, wagons, and artillery and protected from view by the woods. It ran to the southwest and connected to the Plank Road, which went around the exposed Federal flank. Jackson had been convinced of the value of reliable topographical information ever since the Mexican War, and he had used Hotchkiss's knowledge extensively in the Valley. Now it was paying off again, enabling them to find a vital roadway that was uniquely local, just as satellite imagery might be used by a general today to spot an unused path around an enemy position. Such information, delivered in a timely manner, swings the course of battles.

Lee, who had already divided his force once, now took an even larger risk by dividing it a second time. He would leave himself in an inferior position almost identical to the one they had left Jubal Early in at Fredericksburg, staying put with only 14,000 men to pin down Hooker's estimated 50,000 soldiers in their wooded lair. Jackson would lead the remaining force of about 28,000 men and 112 cannon around the end of the Union line to hit the exposed XI Corps.

+≻═≺+

On the road with his troops at about eight o'clock in the morning, Jackson was actually spotted moving south by the Federals. A Union response overran a Georgia brigade, but the Union commanders misread the overall situation and thought the Rebels were retreating. Hooker stalled and went into defensive positions while bringing up reinforcements. He voiced some concern about the western flank, but no one made absolutely sure that it was secured. As the day wore on, Hooker decided to close his trap and sent word back to the force before Fredericksburg to attack there. His main body would pursue the retreating Confederates the following morning.

+≻═≺+

At the end of the woodcutters' road, Jackson pivoted and headed sharply north. The secrecy of the plans and the ability to move a mass of fighting men quickly in a new direction had seldom been so important. It was one of the most dangerous of all military maneuvers, marching almost 30,000 men across the front of an alerted enemy force and having to cover his own flank in the process. Speed was mandatory, and Jackson rode among the soldiers, urging them to hurry on and to stay closed up. An officer said it looked as if the unsmiling Stonewall had the entire plan distinctly imprinted in his mind.

They found the tip of the Union line at about two o'clock in the afternoon. The flank element of the Union corps was facing the wrong way, and its 900 soldiers had stacked their arms and begun to prepare the evening meal. Thinking the dense wood to their right was impenetrable, they had pointed only a few cannons in that direction.

Brigadier General Fitzhugh Lee, a cavalry officer and the nephew of Robert E. Lee, showed the exposed enemy to Jackson from a vantage point, and the general spent a while looking things over. His eyes were lit by a brilliant glow, and his lips were moving. Lee thought, "Oh, beware of rashness, General Hooker. Stonewall Jackson is praying in full view of your right flank."[10]

By the time the sun began to dim, Stonewall Jackson had 18,500 men and most of his artillery in line, the front regiments stretched out in a row two miles long with another line right behind them. The big division of A.P. Hill was still arriving on the field and would serve as the third attack wave and the reserve. Jackson looked at his pocket watch a little after five o'clock and gave the signal to advance. Long gray and brown lines surged into the Wilderness toward the unsuspecting Yankees.

They hit skirmishers, and cavalry units clashed, but Rebel prisoners were ignored when they mocked their captors by warning that a major attack was underway. Through the tangled forest came Jackson's force, briars and limbs tearing skin and uniforms. When several Union colonels hurried back to warn the generals, their claims were also dismissed. Union soldiers cheered the spectacle of animals bursting from the woods and running pell-mell across the open ground. Finally, the Rebel yells could be heard, as the Confederate lines smashed out of the tree line with volleys of musket fire, artillery shells screaming overhead. First the Yankee camp disappeared, then companies, then brigades and regiments, and finally a whole division were gobbled up by the attacking Rebels. Any Yankees putting up resistance was dealt with in minutes, and the rest of the Federal troops packed the few roads as the XI Corps folded in panic. The corps commander, General Oliver Howard, clutching a regimental flag under his amputated arm and weeping at his inability to stop the headlong flight, was swept along by the fleeing soldiers of the Union's evaporated right flank.

General Hooker was on the porch of the Union headquarters in Chancellorsville, listening to what he believed was a Federal attack against Lee, when the mob came flooding past. The general jumped on his horse, grabbed a handy fresh division, and rode west toward the fighting.

The growing darkness brought confusion on both sides, but Jackson was determined to achieve a complete victory before stopping. This was the kind of glorious action that he had always wanted: rolling up an enemy army through an unexpected attack and then pursuing relentlessly. When a young officer yelled to the general that the Yankees were running too fast, Stonewall called back that they could never run too fast for him.

"Never before had his pre-occupation of mind, and his insensibility to danger been so great. At every cheer from the front, which announced some new success, the smile of triumph flashed over his face, followed and banished immediately by the reverential gratitude, with which he raised his face and his right hand to the heavens in prayer and thanksgiving. It was evident that he regarded this as his greatest victory, and never before was he seen so frequently engaged in worship upon the field," wrote early biographer Dabney. [11]

But the attack faltered under the weight of the giant success. Units mingled, and pockets of enemy infantry, cavalry, and artillery stood their ground and regrouped. Riding forward to try and restore order, Jackson gave Hill's division firm orders to continue pressing forward. Jackson nervously roamed the area, keeping in touch with the pulse of the battle until Union artillery found enough range to bring the momentum to a halt.

With some staff members in tow, Jackson went past the advanced picket lines, getting close enough to hear the Yankees chopping trees and giving orders. Behind them was the 18th North Carolina Regiment, which had been on the move or fighting all day and had just finished a scrap with Yankee cavalrymen.

Hill and his immediate staff joined Jackson's group as Stonewall ended his personal reconnoitering, convinced by staffers to leave the exposed forward area. About two dozen horsemen began their return to the safety of the Confederate lines. The Carolinians, nervous beneath the full moon, opened fire at the riders from about 30 yards distance, which seemed to start everybody in the area shooting. Jackson was hit three times and seriously wounded.

One bullet pierced the palm of his right hand, inflicting a wound that proved to be relatively minor despite breaking several small bones. More serious damage was done on his left side, where one bullet went through his arm from elbow to wrist, and a third musket ball crushed the bone just below his left shoulder, breaking the arm and severing an artery. He stayed in the saddle long enough to bring the spooked Little Sorrel under control while others quieted the firing that had killed or wounded 11 members of the group on horseback. Bleeding profusely, staggering along until finally being carried to an ambulance wagon, Jackson had to endure an agonizing trip to the nearest aid station, a number of miles away.

The battle grew intense in the area from which he was pulled, and great sections of the Wilderness were soon aflame, trapped men and animals screaming in the fire. A.P. Hill was wounded in the leg. A soldier carrying Jackson's litter lost both arms to a cannon shot, and the general was spilled onto the ground. Jackson knew he was badly hurt and even thought he was going to die, but he nevertheless remained coherent until doctors anesthetized him to amputate the left arm.

His withdrawal from the front did not mean a stop to the fighting. Jeb Stuart had taken command, but due to the Jackson passion for secrecy, he did not know the overall plan or what strategic and tactical verbal agreements Lee and Stonewall had made between them. Everything was locked in Jackson's head. A messenger was sent to the general, but Jackson was too hurt to impart the information and issue orders. Finally, he said in a weak voice that his cavalryman friend should do what he thought best. The separated Rebel divisions were eventually reunited, and Lee regained control, turned back a Union advance from Fredericksburg, and won the victory when Joe Hooker retreated across the Rappahannock.

Jackson was apparently recovering from the wound over the next few days, and he even began to consider when he might return to duty. Lee needed him. "He has lost his left arm; but I have lost my right arm," Lee said.[12]

Then Jackson developed pneumonia and took a severe turn for the worse. Anna and baby Julia arrived by train; he was able to recognize them, but he fell steadily into a state of delirium, during which he occasionally issued battle orders.

The pious soldier went to his death the same way he fought: sure of his direction, steadfast in his courage, character, and faith, and ready for what he considered the ultimate victory, the moment when he would join his God. Finally, ready to give up his life, the general murmured, "Let us pass over the river, and rest under the shade of the trees."[13]

Lieutenant General Thomas J. "Stonewall" Jackson died at 3:15 P.M. on Sunday, May 10, 1863.

CHAPTER 22

Into the Shade

HIS DEATH WOULD NOT ALTER THE FINAL OUTCOME OF THE CIVIL War. Eventually the strong, resilient, and wealthy North overcame the stubborn, poor South. Talented Union generals, such as Ulysses Grant and Phil Sheridan, came to the fore, and they were fighters.

The central question historians have grappled with is: What would have happened if Stonewall Jackson had not died at Chancellorsville?

One strong school of thought holds that Jackson's successes have been exaggerated, given that he was opposed by such inferior opponents. Grant was one of the first to make this criticism, but many modern generals agree.

Robert E. Lee never wavered in his belief that had Stonewall Jackson been at his side, the South would have won at Gettysburg. Such a critical victory on Northern soil might have led the Union to seek a political rather than a military solution to the war.

The question can give rise to endless speculation, but any answer to it, however interesting, must remain hypothetical.

An even more intriguing question is: How would Jackson have dealt with American wars after his own era? Though no certain answer can be given, we might be able to offer more than just pure speculation, for Jackson's tactics live on even today.

When asked about the enigmatic Civil War leader's legacy to the military world, a prominent modern military historian immediately exclaimed: "Jackson! Why, Chancellorsville! Where do you think that wide left hook in Desert Storm came from?"[1] General H. Normal Schwarzkopf studied Jackson's career extensively while laying his own plans for defeating the army of Iraq.

General Douglas MacArthur was another student of Old Jack, citing him often as an example of leadership. Not only did his gigantic wheeling movement at Inchon in Korea reflect clear Jacksonian influence, but during World War II, he attributed to the Jackson style his idea for small and aggressive landing parties that would hit unsuspecting Japanese forces on Pacific islands.

Eisenhower once described his close battlefield relationship with General Omar Bradley as being similar to the bond between Lee and Jackson.

When Vietnam came along, Stonewall Jackson would have embraced the potential of such a force-multiplying machine as troop-carrying helicopters. A tool like that would have added speed, surprise, and vertical mobility to his striking ability.

But it is hard to imagine Stonewall Jackson functioning in the U.S. Army at any time after the Vietnam era. Jackson thrived on independence of command, and secrecy was his watchword; he would have perished in the modern command fishbowl. He certainly would have preferred to resign on the spot than to tolerate the slightest political interference in how he ran his army. When Jackson was in command, he was in total command, exhibiting a degree of individuality and independence incompatible with the complexities and communications of modern warfare. Today, everybody has to report to somebody else, usually while television is broadcasting the battle in real time to an audience of millions. Although he would have welcomed television and computers as intelligence-gathering tools, he would have detested having Big Brother actually peering over his shoulder as he tried to do his job.

Today's generals and corporate leaders emphasize "lessons learned," a reflective attempt to mine things of value from previous experiences. Jackson left several examples, good and bad, that are applicable in today's world, both civilian and military.

The Personal Touch

The soldiers of the Stonewall Brigade were not supermen—they just thought they were. They believed in Old Jack, he believed in them, and together they believed they could whip anybody, anytime, no matter what the odds. Historians have compared the Stonewall Brigade to the best soldiers ever, troops fielded by the likes of Caesar, Cromwell, and Napoleon. From the first days of recruiting a ragtag force at Harper's Ferry, he set about teaching them how to be soldiers. Long marches and drills every day built endurance and discipline as they learned the harsh realities of war. They marched fast, ignored bad weather, lived on short rations, endured logistical shortages, and overcame adversity. They marched barefoot over icy roads, leaving tracks of their blood in the snow, and they marched beneath the baking summer sun and in clouds of choking dust until they passed out from heat exhaustion. It was a regimen that weeded out the weak, and turned the rest into hard men.

But all the while, they could watch General Jackson constantly working just as hard, and they felt free to strike up a conversation with him. He led by example, and if Jackson could sleep in the cold rain and sit quietly on his horse while gunfire zipped around his ears, they could too. They might not all have liked him, and some thought he was crazy, but he earned their respect. He always refused to commute court-martial executions, arrested anyone who didn't measure up on the field of battle, and demanded exceptional deeds from his men. They struggled to perform these mostly to please him, with astonishing results. After the war, a Confederate veteran's proudest boast was to be able to tell his grandchildren, "I served with Stonewall!"

Tools

In a day when wagons and mules furnished transport, Jackson made certain to "combat load" the supply trains and keep the ammunition wagons at the front. His men could survive longer without rations and warm clothing than they could without ammunition, and there was no point in arriving at a battlefield without being able to shoot. There have been too many instances of the military failing to follow this simple rule, such as the Marines arriving on Guadalcanal with little more than their rifles. When a leader demands great things of people, he or she must give them the tools to do the job.

Create Opportunity

Jackson recognized that it took more than numbers to make an army and he repeatedly nullified the enemy's numerical advantage by gathering intelligence, planning aggressively, moving fast, finding weak points, and following up with unflinching action. He demonstrated that a leader who controls the place and tempo can actually create opportunities where none seemed to exist. The entire Shenandoah campaign was actually nothing but a series of extraordinary diversionary attacks. But by constantly slashing and clawing at the Union forces chasing him through the mountains, Jackson threw enough of a scare into Washington to prevent those forces from going to help strengthen McClellan enough to capture Richmond. Even after the Valley campaign, the mere whisper that Stonewall was on the prowl with his foot cavalry was enough to freeze an enemy general into indecision or push him toward incorrect conclusions. Jackson did not even have to be in a particular place at all to influence events there. Good leaders usually create their own luck.

Find Your Own Weakness

Jackson knew that familiarity with an area was extremely important for a commander, and he acted on this knowledge by hiring Jed Hotchkiss to be his personal mapmaker. Hotchkiss developed into a first-class scout of unknown territory, repeatedly identifying areas that provided Jackson with fast routes, concealment for his troops, and other important tactical advantages. The obscure woodcutters' road Hotchkiss charted with the help of a local guide made all the difference at Chancellorsville.

In a day when massed armies stood toe-to-toe, killing each other at close range and in great numbers, Jackson used his mapmaker's information to maximize his own specialties of movement and surprise. Opposing Union generals described Jackson appearing behind them, or on a flank, or moving quickly to a new position, but virtually never where they wanted him.

+===+

On the downside, Jackson was guilty of being too secret, a flaw that went far beyond securing important military information. He simply did not confide in anyone: not in his wife, his superiors, his friends, or even the fellow generals among his division commanders. Under Jackson, long columns made up of thousands of men, wagons, and horses would trudge for days without the faintest idea where they were heading. "If I thought my coat knew my plans, I would take it off and burn it," said Frederick the Great. Jackson agreed.

In the Piedmont, where he became incapable of making decisions, no one had enough information about Jackson's strategy or goals to step in and take over. At Chancellorsville, when he was shot while the battle was still at a crucial juncture, the other generals had no idea what his orders were. In both situations, the South won victories, but Jackson certainly jeopardized the chances by carrying secrecy to a dangerous extreme.

He used everything at his disposal to create victory, to the point where his personal daring slid into recklessness. His leading from the front would become the stuff of legend, but he was too important to be riding out in the open within musket shot of an entire Yankee column, or advancing to see a blazing front line with his own eyes. His disregard for his own safety ended up costing him his life and the South one of its most talented leaders.

He died at the relatively young age of 38, leaving behind few records of his assessments of particular military situations or the motives behind particular actions. There are no memoirs other than what his letters and formal military communications contain, no speeches, no post-war interviews that might provide clues about what went on inside that brilliant mind. We are forced to rely largely on accounts from those who knew him, a pool significantly narrowed when the war took the lives of such important contemporaries as his West Point classmate, fighting partner, and arch-nemesis, A.P. Hill, and his close friend, cavalry leader Jeb Stuart.

Stonewall Jackson departed life as he had lived it, largely shrouded by mystery.

Notes

Chapter 1

1. The incident is described in G.F.R. Henderson, *Stonewall Jackson and the American Civil War* (New York, Da Capo Press reprint, 1988), 11. Originally published by Grosset & Dunlap, 1943.
2. The family history is detailed on the Jackson Family website http://www.eg.bucknell.edu/~hyde/jackson/.
3. Thomas Jackson, letter to his sister, Laura Arnold, August 2, 1845. Virginia Military Institute Archives.
4. This version of the oft-cited quotation and its antecedents is in John C. Waugh, *The Class of 1846* (New York, Warner Books, 1994), 5.
5. A thorough report on the appointment is found in Byron Farwell, *Stonewall* (New York, W.W. Norton & Company, 1992), 16.
6. Henderson, *Stonewall Jackson,* 9.

Chapter 2

1. Henderson, *Stonewall Jackson,* 11.
2. The incident is frequently cited by biographers such as Farwell, *Stonewall,* 21, and Waugh, *Class of 1846,* 13.
3. Statistical information on West Pointers involved in the Civil War is from the West Point website: http://www.usma.army.mil/bicentennial/history/NotableGrads.asp.
4. Henderson, *Stonewall Jackson,* 15.

Chapter 3

1. James I. Robertson, Jr., *Stonewall Jackson: The Man, The Soldier, The Legend* (New York, Macmillan Publishing USA, 1997), 52. Robertson's work is probably the most comprehensive modern biography of Thomas Jackson.

2. Official report of Commodore David Conner, aboard the U.S.S. *Raritan,* off Sacrificious, to John Y. Mason, Secretary of the Navy, on the landing at Vera Cruz (http:// www.dmwv.org/mexwar/documents/Veracruz.ht).

3. A discussion of multiple sources for this quote is found in Robertson, *Stonewall Jackson,* 61.

4. Farwell, *Stonewall,* 55.

Chapter 4

1. Farwell, *Stonewall,* 60.

2. Robert Leckie, *None Died in Vain* (New York, Harper Perennial, 1991), 324.

3. The figures are found on the website "A Concise History of the U.S.-Mexican War, by Descendants of Mexican War Veterans" (http://www.dmwv.org/mexwar/history/concise.htm, http://www.dmwv.org/mwvets/howto.htm).

Chapter 5

1. Farwell, *Stonewall,* 97.

2. Robertson, *Stonewall Jackson,* 191.

Chapter 6

1. Bill Potter, *Beloved Bride: The Letters of Stonewall Jackson to His Wife* (Vision Forum, Inc., San Antonio, TX, 2002), 31–32.

2. This series of letters is found in Farwell, *Stonewall,* 141–144.

3. Robert Lewis Dabney, *Life and Campaigns of Lieutenant General Thomas J. Stonewall Jackson* (Sprinkle Publications, Harrisonburg, VA, 1983 edition), 185.

4. Potter, *Bride,* 40.

Chapter 7

1. *Battles & Leaders of the Civil War* (Castle Books, New York, Vol. 1, 1956 edition), 122. Brig. Gen. John D. Imboden, "Jackson at Harper's Ferry in 1861."

2. James I. Robertson, Jr., *The Stonewall Brigade* (Louisiana State University Press, Baton Rouge and London, 1977), vii.

3. Waugh, *Class of 1846,* 256.

4. Farwell, *Stonewall,* 166.

Chapter 8

1. Robertson, *Stonewall,* 249.

2. Dabney, *Life and Campaigns,* 204.

3. Potter, *Bride,* 51.

4. Potter, *Bride,* 52.

Chapter 9

1. Richard Wheeler, *Voices of the Civil War* (Thomas Y. Crowell Co., New York, 1976), 31.

2. William Howard Russell, report in the *London Times,* from Wheeler, *Voices,* 34.
3. Farwell, *Stonewall,* 179.
4. There are many accounts of Bee's words, not all at the same. The most accepted version is in Dabney, *Life and Campaigns,* 222.
5. Henderson, *Stonewall Jackson,* 113.
6. Dabney, *Life and Campaigns,* 223.
7. Farwell, *Stonewall,* 194.
8. Dabney, *Life and Campaigns,* 229.

Chapter 10

1. Dabney, *Life and Campaigns,* 278.
2. Robertson, *Stonewall Jackson,* 319.
3. Leckie, *None Died in Vain,* 316.
4. Farwell, *Stonewall,* 226.
5. Robertson, *Stonewall Jackson,* 345.

Chapter 11

1. Farwell, *Stonewall,* 242–243.
2. Robertson, *Stonewall Jackson,* 380
3. Farwell, *Stonewall,* 264.

Chapter 12

1. This frequently cited comment is found in Robert U. Johnson and C.C. Buel, eds., *Battles & Leaders of the Civil War,* four volumes (Castle Books, New York, 1887–88), Vol. II, 297.
2. The incident and all or parts of these quotes are documented in Dabney, *Life and Campaigns,* 379; Henderson, *Stonewall Jackson,* 260; Robertson, *Stonewall Jackson,* 407; and Farwell, *Stonewall,* 292.
3. Bruce Catton, *Centennial History of the Civil War* (Doubleday, Garden City, NY, 1965), Vol. II, Chapter 5, p. 305.

Chapter 13

1. Dabney, *Life and Campaigns,* 397.
2. Letter, Jackson to General Johnston, June 6, 1862, cited in Farwell, *Stonewall,* 316.
3. Henderson, *Stonewall Jackson,* 285.
4. Catton, *Centennial History,* Vol. II, 5, 320.

Chapter 14

1. Robertson, *Stonewall Brigade,* 113.
2. Waugh, *Class of 1846,* 338.
3. Henderson, *Stonewall Jackson,* 350.
4. Farwell, *Stonewall,* 343.

5. William C. Davis, *Battlefields of the Civil War* (Chrysalis Books, London, 2004 edition), 60.
6. K.M. Kostyal, *Stonewall Jackson: A Life Portrait* (Taylor Publishing Company, Dallas, TX, 1999), 136.
7. Farwell, *Stonewall,* 351.
8. Dabney, *Life and Campaigns,* 454

Chapter 15

1. Farwell, *Stonewall,* 361.
2. This comment is traced to a Dabney comment made after the war, cited in Robertson, *Stonewall Jackson,* 495.
3. Catton, *Centennial History,* Vol. II, 5, 337.
4. Dabney, *Life and Campaigns,* 473.
5. Henderson, *Stonewall Jackson,* 401.
6. General George McClellan's *Civil War Papers,* cited in Waugh, *Class of 1846,* 363.
7. As quoted in Henderson, *Stonewall Jackson,* 404.
8. Dabney, *Life and Campaigns,* 501.

Chapter 16

1. Dabney, *Life and Campaigns,* 515.
2. Robertson includes this anecdote in *Stonewall* (550), adding a cautionary note on its origin.
3. Farwell, *Stonewall,* 406.

Chapter 17

1. Leckie, *None Died in Vain,* 355.
2. Kostyal, *Life Portrait,* 162.
3. Farwell, *Stonewall,* 414.

Chapter 18

1. This version of the famous General Order 191 incident is found in Farwell, *Stonewall,* 428.
2. Potter, *Bride,* 105.
3. Dabney, *Stonewall Jackson,* 565.
4. Statistics and quote from the U.S. National Park Service website http://www.nps.gov/archive/anti/battle.htm.

Chapter 19

1. Robertson, *Stonewall Jackson,* 635.
2. Potter, *Bride,* 108.
3. Excellent descriptions of the A.P. Hill complaints are in Farwell, *Stonewall,* 458, and Kostyal, *Life Portrait,* 171.

4. Robertson, *Stonewall Jackson,* 629.
5. Potter, *Bride,* 116–118.

Chapter 20

1. This often quoted Lee statement is found in James Longstreet, *From Manassas to Appomattox* (Philadelphia, 1896), 20.
2. There are several versions of this exchange, including this one cited in Henderson, *Stonewall Jackson,* 579.
3. Robertson, *Stonewall Jackson,* 655.
4. Henderson, *Stonewall Jackson,* 608.
5. Jeff Shaara, *Gods and Generals* (Ballantine Publishing, New York, 1996), 318.
6. Farwell, *Stonewall,* 457.

Chapter 21

1. The family matters cited in these letters are described in Jackson's wintertime correspondence with Anna as cited in Potter, *Bride,* 117–131.
2. Henderson, *Stonewall Jackson,* 634.
3. Leckie, *None Died in Vain,* 426.
4. Various biographies use different versions of this quote, for which several citations are found in Robertson, *Stonewall Jackson,* 701.
5. Potter, *Bride,* 139.
6. Joseph P. Cullen. *Civil War Times Illustrated: The Battle of Chancellorsville* (Harrisburg, PA, Eastern Acorn Press, 1968), 7.
7. A frequently quoted remark; this version is from Leckie, *None Died in Vain,* 437.
8. Farwell, *Stonewall,* 493.
9. Cullen, *Chancellorsville,* 16.
10. Farwell, *Stonewall,* 500.
11. Dabney, *Stonewall Jackson,* 682.
12. Dabney, *Stonewall Jackson,* 716.
13. Dabney, *Stonewall Jackson,* 723.

Chapter 22

1. September 2006 interview with military columnist Joseph L. Galloway, co-author of *We Were Soldiers Once . . . and Young* (Random House, New York, 1992).

Index

DATE			

3/16
8